WHERE IS
PETER RABBIT?

BEATRIX POTTER STUDIES X

Papers presented at
The Beatrix Potter Society Conference
Ambleside, England, August 2002

Text © Elizabeth Booth, Nina Demourova, Bridget Welsh Donaldson, Nicholas Durbridge, Lynne McGeachie, Douglas Martin, Peter Parker, Dale Schafer, Laura C. Stevenson, Kestutis Urba, Shin-ichi Yoshida

This compilation © 2003 The Beatrix Potter Society

Edited by Libby Joy, Judy Taylor

TITLE-PAGE ILLUSTRATION
The Tale of Peter Rabbit, p. 18

FRONT COVER ILLUSTRATION
The Tale of Peter Rabbit, p. 21

BACK COVER ILLUSTRATION
The Tale of Peter Rabbit, frontispiece

ISBN 1 869980 20 4

Typeset and produced by
The Studio Publishing Services Ltd,
Exeter

Contents

Illustration Acknowledgements	4
Introduction	5
Notes on the Contributors	6

'A Vogue for Small Books': The Tale of Peter Rabbit and its
Contemporary Competitors
    LAURA C. STEVENSON   11

The Typographic Adventures of The Tale of Peter Rabbit
    DOUGLAS MARTIN   28

The Frederick Warne Archive and Beatrix Potter
    ELIZABETH BOOTH   43

The Challenge of Reading Beatrix Potter
    Reading Beatrix Potter in the UK
        LYNNE McGEACHIE   54
    Reading Beatrix Potter in the United States
        DALE SCHAFER   59
    Developing Children's Responses to the 'Little Books' Using Worksheets
        BRIDGET WELSH DONALDSON   63

Beatrix Potter Overseas
    Peter Rabbit in Russia
        NINA DEMOUROVA   69
    A Case of Distortions
        SHIN-ICHI YOSHIDA   75
    The Perils Peter Rabbit Has Faced in Lithuania
        KESTUTIS URBA   79

Beatrix Potter's Side Shows
    NICHOLAS DURBRIDGE   86

Gardening with Beatrix Potter
    PETER PARKER   96

Index   110

Illustration Acknowledgements

The Beatrix Potter Society is grateful to the following for permission to reproduce illustrations:

National Trust, pp. 48, 49
Private Collection, pp. 51
Frederick Warne & Co: front cover, *The Tale of Peter Rabbit* p. 21 © 1902, 2002; back cover, *The Tale of Peter Rabbit* frontispiece © 1902, 2002; title-page, *The Tale of Peter Rabbit* p. 18 © 1902, 2002; page 34, *The Tale of Timmy Tiptoes* p. 22 © 1911; page 36, *The Tale of Peter Rabbit* © 1902, 2002; page 37, *The Tale of Peter Rabbit* © 1902, 2002; page 41, *The Tale of Peter Rabbit* © 1902, 1987, 2002; page 47, *The Tale of Peter Rabbit* p. 22 © 1902, 2002; page 48 (left), *The Tale of Pigling Bland* p. 21 © 1913, 2002; page 48 (right), *The Tale of Benjamin Bunny* p. 25 © 1904, 2002; page 50 (left) © 1955; page 50 (right), *The Tale of Squirrel Nutkin* p. 21 © 1903, 2002; page 78 (right), *The Tailor of Gloucester* p. 49 © 1903, 2002; page 85, *The Tale of Peter Rabbit* jacket © 1902, 1987; page 88, *Peter Rabbit's Painting Book* © 1911, 2002; page 97 (left) © 1903; page 97 (right), *The Tale of Benjamin Bunny* p. 34 © 1904, 2002; page 99 © 1909; page 101 © 1891; page 102 © 1955; page 103, *The Tale of Mr. Jeremy Fisher* p. 17 © 1906, 2002; page 105, *The Tale of Tom Kitten* frontispiece © 1907, 2002; page 107, *The Tale of Jemima Puddle-Duck* p. 21 © 1908, 2002; page 108, *Cecily Parsley's Nursery Rhymes* p. 29 © 1922, 2002

Introduction

For every International Study Conference the Beatrix Potter Society selects a theme, and the choice for 2003 was made amid the celebrations for the centenary of Frederick Warne's publication of Beatrix Potter's *The Tale of Peter Rabbit*. For one hundred years this author's first and most loved character had been shared by millions, not only in book form but also in many other guises. So the question was asked 'Where next, Peter Rabbit?' As it turned out, the Conference did not really answer the question – which was probably just as well. However, as you will see from this collection of the papers that were given in August 2003, the programme was wide-ranging and of considerable interest, perhaps more concerned with the past and present of Peter Rabbit, with only an occasional hint to his future.

Laura C. Stevenson examined the children's book scene at the time of *The Tale of Peter Rabbit*'s publication, expertly placing it among its contemporaries and suggesting that we should 'view Peter's future in an historical perspective'. The typographer and book designer *Douglas Martin* took us carefully through his redesigning of the little books for the Centenary Editions 'with the benefit of our more sophisticated resources', revealing the extraordinary detail involved in the making of a book (and we strongly advise you to have a set of the new editions beside you when you read his piece). The archivist, *Elizabeth Booth*, introduced the database for the Frederick Warne digital archive, explaining how the artwork, letters, photographs and 'articles of memorabilia' were categorised and indexed, and are being brought to the public in a new way. A panel reported on the origins and the work of the Society's fast-growing *Reading Beatrix Potter* project, *Lynne McGeachie* covering the UK and *Dale Schafer* the USA, and *Bridget Welsh Donaldson* discussed her design of the scheme's worksheets. As a result, we can guarantee that Peter Rabbit will appear in many more schools and libraries in the coming years. A second panel entertainingly revealed their personal experiences and difficulties of translating Beatrix Potter's books into their respective languages and expressed their hopes for more translations in the future, *Nina Demourova* into Russian, *Shin-ichi Yoshida* into Japanese and *Kestutis Urba* into Lithuanian.

The merchandising of Beatrix Potter's characters is not new but the proliferation of today's merchandise is bemusing. *Nicholas Durbridge* took a swift tour through the history of the merchandise and some of the products on offer to today's customers – a licensing programme that 'is set to run and run'.

Finally *Peter Parker* led the reader into Beatrix Potter's gardens, identifying the profusion of plants and flowers to be found there – and sometimes taking a close look at the people.

In transferring the talks into published form, the editors have retained the American spelling of those from that country and have printed footnotes if supplied. As the number in its sub-title denotes, although this is the tenth volume of Beatrix Potter Society Studies it will certainly not be the last. There is an inexhaustible mine of information still to be quarried about this fascinating woman.

Notes on the Contributors

Elizabeth Booth began her career in 1979 as a bilingual secretary working in the International Advertisement Department of *The Guardian*. When she realised that the editor's job was already taken, she embarked on successive unsuccessful attempts to take over several different organisations, including the Wigmore Hall, the Readers' Digest and the Arts Council (drama department). Having exhausted herself thus far, she finally set her sights on more modest ambitions, including a career in book publishing, working first as editor's secretary at *The Bookseller*, where she learned to use a fax machine while witnessing the founding of The Groucho Club. In 1986 she moved to Frederick Warne & Co. where she remained until 2002, fulfilling multiple roles including making tea for Roger McGough, building the Frederick Warne Archive into an important research resource for scholars, and developing a programme of art exhibitions to bring children's literature and Beatrix Potter's clogs to the public. Her experiences provide material for her current work as a writer and visiting university lecturer in cultural industries marketing, and serve as motivation, interest and threats for her students, at undergraduate and postgraduate level. She maintains an active interest in the world of Beatrix Potter research because she enjoys the custard cream biscuits that the Society serves at its meetings and hopes that one day she might uncover the real Beatrix Potter.

Nina M. Demourova graduated from Moscow State University (English department) and has taught there, and at Moscow State Pedagogical University and the Russian Open University, lecturing on English and American children's literature, translation, stylistics and text analysis. Her doctorate was on English children's literature 1750–1870. She is now Professor of the

University of the Russian Academy of Education, specialising in translation, criticism and advice to Russian publishers on contemporary British children's literature, with an emphasis on issues previously neglected in Russia – children with problems (drugs, bullying, suicide, etc), tolerance, children with special needs, children and war. She has compiled and edited two series of books on these subjects. Nina has lectured in Great Britain, USA, Australia and New Zealand, and her many translations include books by Dickens, Carroll, Hodgson Burnett, Barrie, MacDonald and Garner, and stories by Farjeon, Mahy, Dahl. She translated the Russian editions of *The Tale of Mrs. Tiggy-Winkle*, *The Tale of Mrs. Tittlemouse*, *The Tale of Tom Kitten*, *The Tale of Two Bad Mice*, *The Tale of Squirrel Nutkin* and *The Tale of Timmy Tiptoes*. Her other Potter translations still await a good publisher.

Bridget Welsh Donaldson grew up in Burton upon Trent. At the University of York she took a degree in Language and Education, studying children's literature and qualifying as a teacher specialising in English. Her first teaching post in 1982 was in Manchester and four years later she returned to the Staffordshire/Derbyshire borders, where she still teaches in primary schools. Joining The Beatrix Potter Society in 1998, she soon became a Reader in the *Reading Beatrix Potter* project. This inspired her to design a range of worksheets for developing children's responses to the stories, which have been approved by Frederick Warne and are used by Readers in the UK and the USA. She enjoys sharing her Beatrix Potter interest with her husband and three children, especially on their frequent visits to the Lake District. The family live close to the Peak District and when they are not looking after their Grade II Listed cottage, its garden, a cat, two rabbits and three guinea-pigs, they like to go walking and cycling.

Nicholas Durbridge is Chairman and CEO of The Copyrights Group Limited, which he founded with Linda Pooley in 1984. Prior to Copyrights he was a practising solicitor specialising in media and copyright work. He first became involved in merchandise licensing when one of his clients, Michael Bond, the creator of Paddington Bear, asked him to run the licensing programme for that famous character. Copyrights has now grown to be one of the largest international licensing agencies in the world and specialises in representing classic children's literature, fine art and brand names. As well as Peter Rabbit, Copyrights represents Paddington Bear, The Snowman, Spot, Maisy and the Flower Fairies. Nicholas lives in North Oxfordshire and has two daughters, a son and a stepson.

Lynne McGeachie has climbed and walked in Scotland and the Lake District for over thirty years in all weathers and at every season of the year and, like Beatrix Potter, she has a passion for wild, unspoilt places. She shares this love of the hills with her husband, Gibson. Both are 'Munroists', having climbed together, accompanied by their faithful Border Collies, the Scottish peaks of 3,000 feet and over, known as Munros. This in turn has inspired Lynne to write poetry and she has had work published in *The Scottish Mountaineering Club Journal* and in *Cumbria*. She has also given illustrated lectures to schools on the joy and inspiration of mountaineering and ski touring in her native landscape and on the importance of protecting and conserving that landscape. In addition to the life of Beatrix Potter, her other interests include history and the history of mountaineering, wildlife and photography. She is the UK Reading Organiser for *Reading Beatrix Potter*.

Douglas Martin acts as design consultant to several publishers at any given time, and in the children's-book field cherishes his long associations with Brockhampton Press and latterly with Julia MacRae; he currently enjoys working regularly with Mathew Price and with Barn Owl Books. Major publishers have come to him with one-off projects which have ranged from the deceptive simplicity of Beatrix Potter's 'little books' to the accreted complexities of *Whitaker's Almanack*. Working with the leading illustrators led to his first book *The Telling Line: Essays on fifteen contemporary book illustrators* (1989) and to his biography of *Charles Keeping* (1993). He curated the exhibition *The World of English Picture Books* which toured Japan in 1998-9. His life-long interest in Gutenberg and early printing led to an English translation of Albert Kapr's *Johann Gutenberg: The Man and his Invention*, and he is the translator of Stephan Füssel's *Gutenberg and the Impact of Printing*.

Peter Parker is the author of *The Old Lie: The Great War and the Public-School Ethos* (1987) and a biography of J.R. Ackerley (1989). He is the editor of *A Reader's Guide to the Twentieth-Century Novel* (1995) and *A Reader's Guide to Twentieth-Century Writers* (1996). His authorised biography of Christopher Isherwood will be published in 2004. He is an associate editor of the *New Dictionary of National Biography*, with responsibility for modern literature, and has served on various committees, including PEN and the London Library. Since 1979 he has been a regular contributor of book reviews and features to numerous newspapers and magazines in England and America. He currently reviews fiction for *The Sunday Times* and writes about gardening for *The Daily Telegraph* and *Hortus*. He was elected a Fellow of the Royal Society of

Literature in 1997. Born on a Herefordshire farm, he now lives and gardens in London's East End.

Dale Schafer taught second through sixth grades for thirty-three years in California, before retiring in early 2001, though she continues to teach fourth and fifth graders writing and keyboarding. As a representative for the AlphaSmart Company (word processors for schools), Dale trains teachers in their use. She is also a consultant, giving writing workshops to school districts in the Southern California area. She is listed in *Who's Who Among America's Teachers* for 1992 and 2002, a special honour as the nominations were from her past high school students. Dale's interest in Beatrix Potter started as a child and continued into her teaching career. She used Beatrix Potter's books in her teaching and continues to do so when helping children with their reading and writing. She joined the Society in 1993 and has attended all Conferences since, presenting a paper in 1998 called 'How Beatrix Potter's Childhood Reading Influenced her Writing Style', based on her own interest in Beatrix Potter and her students' learning style. Since 1999 she has been the Society's US West Coast Liaison Officer, and in 2001 she became the *Reading Beatrix Potter* Organizer for the USA.

Laura Stevenson is a Professor of Writing and Humanities at Marlboro College, in Marlboro, Vermont, where she has taught since 1986. For many years, her academic speciality was Elizabethan history and literature; after spending 1982–3 as an Andrew W. Mellon Faculty Fellow at Harvard, she published *Praise and Paradox: Merchants and Craftsmen in Elizabethan Literature*. In 1984, facing escalating deafness, she moved to Vermont, where she began to write children's fiction. Her books for children include *Happily After All* (1990), *The Island and the Ring* (1991), *All the King's Horses* (2001), and *A Castle in the Window* (2003). She is currently writing a book about Beatrix Potter and five other Victorian and Edwardian children's authors, a project funded in part by a research grant from the National Endowment for the Humanities.

Kestutis Urba was born in Kelme, Lithuania, in 1954. He studied Lithuanian Language and Literature at Vilnius University, graduating in 1978. He became a Doctor of Humanities there in 1986 and Assistant Professor in 1989. Since 1978 he has taught at Vilnius University, where he is now an Assistant Professor, and where he was Dean of the Faculty of Philology from 1989 to 1997. His subjects include Lithuanian Literature, Children's Literature and the Teaching of Literature. Kestutis Urba is President of the

Lithuanian section of IBBY (International Board on Books for Young People) and editor of *Rubinaitis*, a children's literary criticism magazine. He has published a number of works on children's literature and, as well as translating four of Beatrix Potter's little books, has translated a number of children's books into Lithuanian, including titles by Mary Norton, Michael Bond and Frances Hodgson Burnett.

Shin-ichi Yoshida was born in Tokyo in 1931. He taught at Rikkyo University in Tokyo, where he is now a Professor Emeritus, and also at the Japan Women's University in Tokyo. He has served as President of the Japan Society for Children's Literature in English, and also as the first President of Ehon-gakkai (picture-book study) Associates. He visited the United Kingdom and met Leslie Linder just before the publication of *A History of the Writings of Beatrix Potter* in 1971, and made his first tour of places connected with Beatrix Potter on Mr Linder's advice. He has published several books on Beatrix Potter in Japan – *Letters from Peter Rabbit* (1990), *The World of Peter Rabbit* (1994) and the Japanese versions of Judy Taylor's *Beatrix Potter: Artist, Storyteller and Countrywoman* and Elizabeth Buchan's *Beatrix Potter: the Story of the Creator of Peter Rabbit*, both in 2001.

'A Vogue for Small Books':
The Tale of Peter Rabbit and its Contemporary Competitors

LAURA C. STEVENSON

TO DISCUSS Peter Rabbit's future is to discuss the fate of a picture book in a world full of television, movies, and video games that compete with children's reading time. It is fashionable to lament these tempting activities and the commercialism that profits from them; but without approving for an instant of the greed with which adults adulterate the innocence of the innocent, I think that it is important to view Peter's future in an historical perspective.

From the very moment it was first printed, *The Tale of Peter Rabbit* had to compete for children's attention, not only with bicycles, penny dreadfuls, golliwog dolls, and pantomimes, but with an impressive body of children's literature. Peter's tale shares its centennial with some 450 other children's books, among them Rudyard Kipling's *Just So Stories*, E. Nesbit's *Five Children and It*, and the dramatic version of Frances Hodgson Burnett's *A Little Princess*. Once a book becomes a classic, its success seems inevitable, so we tend to forget the competitive nature of the late Victorian and early Edwardian publishing world. But we should not. Nor should we forget that to Beatrix Potter – whose nature was a kind of three-color process in which great practical intelligence, sensitive artistic observation and deep social shyness combined to create a wide spectrum of personal characteristics – competition was not just an abstract entity. By her own admission, she decided to publish *The Tale of Peter Rabbit* because it was as good as other books coming out.

This admission has received little attention because of the context in which it appeared – in an article entitled ' "Roots" of the Peter Rabbit Tales', published in *The Horn Book* of 1929. It was Beatrix Potter's only formal

11

autobiographical statement for she saw no reason to amplify it: 'It is frank and downright;' she wrote in 1942, 'but accurate.'[1] The essay *is* frank, and it *is* accurate, but it is also a post-Romantic portrait of an artist as carefully crafted as any of the backgrounds in the little books.[2] At Peter's roots, Beatrix says, lies her own descent from 'generations of Lancashire yeomen and weavers' – non-industrialized country people. More directly, his roots lie in Beatrix's pastoral childhood, 'a good deal' of which was spent in the Highlands of Scotland, nurtured by the folktales of a highland nurse who believed 'in witches, fairies and the creed of the terrible John Calvin (the creed rubbed off, but the fairies remained)'.

Peter's literary roots lie in Beatrix's childhood reading: the novels of Sir Walter Scott and Maria Edgeworth and *not*, she emphasizes, a 'stodgy fat book – I think it was called a *History of the Robin Family*, by Mrs Trimmer', which she hated. The target here is not the book, but the infamous Mrs Trimmer, who as editor of *The Guardian of Education* in 1802–6, had successfully eradicated fairy-tales from children's reading for fifty years. Finally, Peter's roots were free of the conformity of schooling: 'Thank goodness, my education was neglected; I was never sent to school . . . it would have rubbed off some of the originality.' Original insight, free from industrial and intellectual pollution, nurtured by the countryside and its people – at Peter's roots lie the artistic ideals of Wordsworth and Ruskin.

As for *The Tale of Peter Rabbit* itself, she continues, it was written for a real child whose illness prompted a letter 'with pen and ink scribbles'. But when she tried to publish the story, it met with bourgeois indifference:

> After a time there began to be a vogue for small books, and I thought "Peter" might do as well as some that were being published. But I did not find any publisher who agreed with me. The manuscript – nearly word for word the same, but with only outline illustrations – was returned with or without thanks by at least six firms. Then I drew my savings out of the post office savings bank, and got an edition of 450 copies printed.

After selling the private edition to obliging aunts, she adds, she showed it to Warne, and the rest, of course, is history – original, non-commercial, genuine art triumphed.

It is easy to read over the sentence about the 'vogue for small books', because in its post-Romantic context, it compares original art to a commercial fad. But this sentence – and, indeed, the whole brief story of Peter's publication – had appeared previously in a letter Beatrix had written to Anne Carroll Moore in 1925, when *The Horn Book* first asked her for her autobiography. In *both* versions, Beatrix says quite candidly that what prompted her to attempt publication was 'a fashion for little picture books' or 'a vogue for small books' that made her think – in the significantly more competitive phrase of the later statement – ' "Peter" might do as well as some that were being published'. It appears that some little books she saw in shops, or when she visited Noel Moore and his siblings, made her think of publishing a letter she had written seven years earlier. So the question naturally arises, was there indeed a vogue for little books – and if so, which of those books became a catalyst for Peter's publication?

Little books were certainly not unusual in Victorian England. Miniature books had appeared as early as the fifteenth century, and after the Reformation miniature Bibles were very popular, beginning a long history of small religious works. Most familiar in the mid-nineteenth century were the tracts with which evangelical presses deluged the market. But sermons and devotional literature were usually small, too: to reach a wide audience, books had to be cheap, and paper was expensive. The dictates of economy often ensured that children's literature – beginning with John Newbery's books – was printed in small format. And of course, there were size fads. In 1807, William Roscoe's charming picture book, *The Butterfly's Ball*, was followed by dozens of little imitators.

Victorian novels, however, were printed in a large, expensive format – the three-decker, which cost 31s. The assumption – in 1888 as in 1828 – was that nobody bought them entire: middle-class people either read them in periodicals or borrowed them from Mudie's Circulating Library. By the mid-nineteenth century, however, rising literacy in the lower classes increased demand for inexpensive reading material, and cheaper paper and high-speed presses made it technologically possible to meet that demand; thus presses began to bring out series like Routledge's Pocket Library, which reprinted popular novels in a small format – and very small print. The format was successful, but it had an accidental social connotation: to most Victorians between 1845 and 1890, possession of a small volume suggested either an evangelical bent or an implied admission that one was not respectably middle class. There were exceptions, of course: the small almanacs Kate Greenaway put out yearly enjoyed a vogue in the 1880s and 1890s. But they were aesthetic ephemera, not real reading.

As with adult works, so with children's. In the 1850s, the competition of penny dreadfuls forced the religious presses, which by then did most children's publishing, to change both what and how they published. Child deaths and the imports and exports of Peru gave way to the wholesome adventure stories and domestic fiction of Ballantyne, Henty, Mrs Ewing and Mrs Molesworth, which were published first in folio magazines, then in 6s quartos. The sizes and prices were unaffected by the religious presses' loss of their monopoly the year before

Beatrix Potter was born, when Macmillan published Lewis Carroll's *Alice's Adventures in Wonderland* and Charles Kingsley's *The Water-Babies*. Though this event, and the passage of the Education Act five years later, made it clear to commercial presses that children's publishing was becoming too lucrative to leave to the religious, all presses packaged their children's literature in the same brightly-colored quartos. And so it was that the children's books Beatrix Potter remembered with affection – Mrs Molesworth's *Carrots* and Dinah Mulock's *Little Sunshine* – were both of standard size, and that her beloved Caldecott picture books were large and oblong.

The status of little books changed during the 1890s, during most of which the Peter Rabbit letter sat quietly in Noel Moore's drawer. The change was part of a new attention to book format that burst upon the publishing world in 1891, when William Morris founded the Kelmscott Press. Morris had, of course, long advocated the beautiful and well constructed rather than the cheap and ugly, but his press forced other publishers to face the tacit accusation that mass-produced books fell into the latter category. It was not just a matter of ornamentation. Looking back on his beginnings as an 1890s publisher, Grant Richards asserted that Kelmscott's primary contribution to the trade was the revival of attractive layout. Morris insisted:

Frontispiece and title-page of William Morris, *The Wood Beyond the World*, decorated by Sir Edward Burne-Jones, The Kelmscott Press, 1894

... that when one opened a book one should see the two printed pages as one whole and not as two, that the inner margins should hardly be greater than was rendered necessary by the requirements of the binder, and that the outer and bottom margins should much exceed those at the top. The thing was overdone, but the principle was right, and the Kelmscott convention profoundly influenced the printers who were not too hide-bound to cast off a bad habit. . . . [They] went back to the balance and proportion of the old manuscript books and to the books of the artist-craftsmen who had followed the birth of printing.[3]

The difficulty for publishers who wished to associate themselves with 'the artist-craftsmen' of earlier eras was, of course, producing beautiful books cheaply; but here they were assisted by a variety of trends. One of them was the late Victorian vogue for fairy-tales. In 1888, Oscar Wilde's *The Happy Prince and Other Tales*, illustrated in part by Walter Crane, had established the beautifully produced literary fairy-tale as a popular aesthetic mode. Andrew Lang, who had little use for aestheticism, had retaliated the next year with *The Blue Fairy Book*, traditional tales collected by his wife and daughter but published under his name. Its popularity established not only a series of 'color fairy books' but also a series of imitators. And the imitators were not limited to fairy tales; Frazer's *The Golden Bough*, which appeared in 1890, triggered a demand for folklore and mythology. Thus, at the time when the Kelmscott Press was founded, fairy-tales and myths had become 'crossover' in every sense of the term. They could be marketed for children, with the knowledge they would also be bought by aesthetes, Tennyson-lovers, scholars, romantically-inclined women, and repentant agnostics – the list was endless. This was a publisher's dream, for neither fairy-tales nor myths were copyrighted.

Fairy-tales and legends lent themselves to the black-and-white decoration that the Kelmscott Press made fashionable; and here again, the publishers were lucky. The use of photography in the engraving process in the 1860s and 1870s had led in the 1880s to faster, less expensive means of reproducing illustrators' drawings: line block, half-tone block, and etching. Accommodating the resulting explosion in demand for black-and-white illustration, a new generation of illustrators was pouring out of art schools, talented, eager, and cheap.

Given these coinciding trends, it is not surprising that one of the first series of books influenced by the Kelmscott Press was George Unwin's twelve-volume Children's Library, which appeared from 1891 to 1894. This was a series of handsomely-bound little books which included, among others, Giambattista Basile's *Pentamerone*, the first English translation of Carlo Collodi's *Pinocchio* and Ernst Beckman's *Max and Carlino*, the last illustrated by Florence Upton. No doubt thoughts of copyright influenced the international selection, but that selection was enterprising – and, more important, the Kelmscott beauty of the set's small format made it clear to other publishers that little books, in addition to being cheap to produce, could be fashionable.

There were publishers more than ready to learn this lesson. The 1890s saw the advent of a publishing generation that had grown up as autodidacts during the aesthetic era, and had first-hand knowledge of the audience that sought both beauty and education in books. Chief among these was John Lane, who joined with Charles Elkin Mathews in 1889 to found The Bodley Head. Lane quickly became a self-appointed literary arbiter who 'defined for book buyers for the period what constituted "elegant" appearance and sophisticated content'.[4] He defined 'elegant appearance' in his series The Flowers of Parnassus, collections of famous poems beautifully illustrated by the new generation of artists. As for 'sophisticated content', Lane began The Keynote Series, which offered prose works in progressive, anti-Victorian voices. The volumes in both these series were sold for a shilling, and Lane reduced production costs in the time-honored way: printing uncopyrighted poetry, and grossly underpaying his authors and illustrators. But he also chose a format half the size of a standard octavo. As a result of his success, exciting new ideas (or great poetry with exciting new illustrations) quickly became associated with nicely crafted little books.

In the year that Lane began The Keynote Series – which was, incidentally, also the year in which Beatrix Potter wrote the Peter Rabbit letter – another fledgling publisher, J. M. Dent, took up the Kelmscott challenge by bringing out a beautiful edition of Malory's *Le Morte D'Arthur*, illustrated by a nineteen-year-old insurance clerk named Aubrey Beardsley. And if it was Lane who realized what could be done with Aubrey Beardsley, it was Dent who realized what could be done with little books in a mass market. Eventually, this realization led to the Everyman Library. But in 1894, it led to The Temple Shakespeare, a series that soon ran to forty volumes. Because of Lane's competition, each attractively-designed volume cost a shilling, and each was small. The Temple Shakespeare, which in the next forty years sold five million copies, was almost exactly the size of the later published *The Tale of Peter Rabbit*.

In 1894, then, the vogue for small books was well begun. Dent, encouraged by Beardsley's success, found other aspiring young artists to launch (or exploit, depending on one's point of view) and extended the new fashion to the crossover market Unwin had attracted. The result was the Banbury Cross Series: twelve tiny volumes of fairy-tales and nursery rhymes at 1s a volume, 13s 6d a boxed set. It was a stunning series. The young artists Dent had chosen later became well-known illustrators; among them were R. Anning Bell,

H. Granville Fell and Charles Robinson. Nor did he limit the opportunities he offered to men: *The House that Jack Built* was illustrated by Violet Holden, and *Banbury Cross and other Nursery Rhymes* was illustrated by Alice Woodward, whose sister helped Beatrix Potter print *The Tale of Peter Rabbit* privately.

At the time these books came out, Beatrix was also becoming a professional illustrator, but she was working in entirely different publishing circles. Her editors at Hildesheimer & Faulkner and Ernest Nister produced ingenious toy books with moving parts, cards and sentimental books with chromolithographed color pictures, cheaply printed in Germany. Working for them was nothing to be ashamed of; Beatrix's description of her first meeting with Mr Faulkner may show that she knew Grub Street when she saw it – but she also admitted that one of the press's artists drew animals better than she did and noted her uncle's comment that he had seen nothing vulgar.[5] That is a fair comment on both presses. The illustrations in Nister's books were well done, particularly in those edited by Robert Ellice Mack, the man with whom Beatrix Potter haggled about the price for her series 'A Frog he would a-fishing go'.

'How King Arthur saw the Questing Beast', Aubrey Beardsley's frontispiece to Sir Thomas Malory, *Le Morte D'Arthur*, Vol. 1, J.M. Dent, 1893

But working for Grub Street was a matter of money, not of art. Nister produced what the public wanted, and his public (unlike Beardsley's) wanted predictable novelty – happy endings, sorrowful partings, tongue-in-cheek humor, cute puppies and kittens, adorable children – in an attractive format. Sometimes this format included size: in 1890, for example, Nister produced a boxed set of miniature books called *The Little Folks' Favourite Library*. On the surface it is pretty; closer inspection reveals that the print is minuscule and that in any given story the pictures have nothing in common except their subjects – the kittens on page one, for example, may be replaced by entirely different kittens on page two. This oddity is easily explainable, for Nister's illustrators did not illustrate: they submitted pictures which Mack sorted by theme (kittens, puppies, farms and so on) and sent to trusted writers to make into stories. In this case, the writer was E. Nesbit, who at that time was working for Mack. Nesbit's friend Alice Hoatson often helped her, and she remembered their Grub Street days as follows:

> Sheaves of illustrations used to be sent down to us and we wrote stories and verse to these pictures . . . [We began at] about 10.30 p.m. and . . . wrote till far into the night. Our inspiration was weak gin and water – very shocking! One tablespoon each, in water, was our allowance but sometimes E. would say 'Oh, Mouse, just one more and we can get this batch done. Mack wants it done at once.'[6]

The text accompanying Beatrix Potter's 'A Frog he would a-fishing go', which appeared in *Nister's Holiday Annual* the year Dent's Banbury Cross series was published, was most likely produced under analogous circumstances.

The lovely illustrations of *Cinderella* or *Brer Rabbit* that Beatrix Potter drew at this time suggest that she had aspirations beyond Grub Street, but it was difficult to move from Nister to other presses. E. Nesbit, who counted among her friends Richard Le Gallienne, Laurence Housman and George Bernard Shaw, and whose progressive ideas (and extraordinary beauty) led John Lane to print some of her work, had a way out. But Beatrix Potter did not move in such circles – and, importantly, she was illustrating in color and thinking in terms of Caldecott at a time when Beardsley was all the rage. So it is not surprising that while her desire for independence kept her sending work to Nister in 1894 and 1895, the artist in her increasingly turned to 'drawing funguses very hard'. Natural history looked like a real hope, and may have continued to do so even after the non-reception of her paper at the Linnaean Society in 1897 – Roy Watling has reminded us that she produced at least sixty-seven fungus paintings after the meeting.[7] But by late 1899, it was becoming clear that her beautiful mycological works were not going to be 'put in a book' someday.[8] And that is when, by her own authority, a vogue for little picture books turned her thoughts to publishing *The Tale of Peter Rabbit*.

The publishing world to which she returned was crucially different from the one she had left. During her four-year absence, William Morris and Sir Edmund Burne-Jones had died, and the Kelmscott Press shortly thereafter. Aubrey Beardsley had also died, still in his twenties; Oscar Wilde, now a ruined man, was dying in Paris. It was a time for new voices, and some of the best-known of those voices were speaking to children. Rudyard Kipling's *The Jungle Book* and *The Second Jungle Book* had become classics; *The Golden Age* and *Dream Days* had made Kenneth Grahame a famous name; and E. Nesbit's

The Treasure Seekers was making her fortune. But the great children's publishing phenomena were the golliwog books, which began with *The Adventures of Two Dutch Dolls and a 'Golliwogg'* in 1895, and continued in twelve sequels until 1909. These books, in which doggerel verses by Ruth Upton faced color illustrations by her daughter Florence, used the familiar large oblong format of Caldecott's toy books. But the bright, poster-style illustrations – and, perhaps more importantly, the unstructured white areas that surrounded them – greatly influenced the picture book as we know it today.

The other publishing phenomenon that had appeared during Beatrix's absence was Grant

The Golliwog books (1895–1909), by Ruth and Frances Upton

Richards, a well-connected young man who set up his press in 1897 and became, in the next four years, the publisher of George Bernard Shaw, A. E. Housman, G. K. Chesterton and Saki. Grudgingly respectful of Morris's influence and determined that his books 'were to look at least as well as those of [his] competitors',[9] he looked at those competitors' works carefully. He noticed that the success of the Children's Library and the Banbury Cross Series had prompted other presses to issue small editions of their most popular children's authors. But he also saw that nobody had brought out a prestigious series of little children's books. So he started one: The Dumpy Books For Children.

The series was well reviewed, and critics especially appreciated the small size of the volumes, but Richards lost money on it. Then, in 1899, he was shown a small picture-book manuscript called *The Story of Little Black Sambo*, which a Scottish woman named Helen Bannerman, living in India with her surgeon husband, had written for her two- and five-year-old daughters – and, alas, had sent to England in the care of a friend who knew nothing about the publishing industry. To coerce the friend into selling the copyright for £5 was child's play for Richards; and *The Story of Little Black Sambo* came out in

October 1899 as Dumpy Book Number 4. The return was probably the largest of Richards' publishing career. Reviewers raved. The first edition sold out in a month, necessitating a second; a third sold out for the Christmas market of 1900; the fourth claimed there were 21,000 copies in print.[10]

Without a doubt, it was *The Story of Little Black Sambo* that provoked Beatrix Potter to think ' "Peter" might do as well as some [little books] that were being published'. It was the only *little* picture book coming out around 1900 – and it was revolutionary. Between its fashionably small covers, it offered a story to very young children, with a few words of simple, non-moralistic text facing brightly-colored pictures. Even more than the golliwog books, it defined what the picture book would become. But it is not hard to see why *The Story of Little Black Sambo*'s popularity would arouse a competitive spirit in a woman who valued artistic originality; for the book was entirely derivative. Sambo himself was the Bannerman girls' golliwog doll – a private reference that linked his public reception to that of Florence and Ruth Upton's books.[11] The tigers Sambo encountered evoked Kipling's two *Jungle Books*. As for the illustrations, they were an amateurish cross between Florence Upton's and those of the mid-century best-seller *Struwwelpeter*. To be fair, the story's inherent charm transcends its derivative roots. But that charm was doubtless lost on an unpublished author who had written an original, beautifully-illustrated story for the same age group.

By mid-March 1900 – five months after *The Story of Little Sambo*'s appearance – Beatrix had made the Peter Rabbit letter into a dummy book, and she was negotiating with a publisher. Her letter to Noel Moore's sister Marjorie (Marjory) makes it clear she had a little-book format and price in mind:

> The publisher is a gentleman who prints books, and he wants a bigger book than he has got enough money to pay for! and Miss Potter has arguments with him. He was taken ill on Sunday and his sisters and his cousins and his aunts had arguments, I wonder if that book will ever be printed! I think Miss Potter will go off to another publisher soon! She would rather make 2 or 3 little books costing 1/- each, than one big book costing 6/- because she thinks little rabbits cannot afford to spend 6 shillings on one book, and would never buy it.[12]

Nor was she thinking of just *any* little book. For the dummy book of *The Tale of Peter Rabbit* she did not choose the 1890s format of the Banbury Cross books, in which the illustrations encircled the text, nor of a *Little Folks' Favourite*, in which the text wove between pictures – but of the little picture-book style that Bannerman had used in *The Story of Little Black Sambo*.

We come now to her difficulties, which I think can be attributed at least in part to factors other than true art rejected. One of these factors appears in the

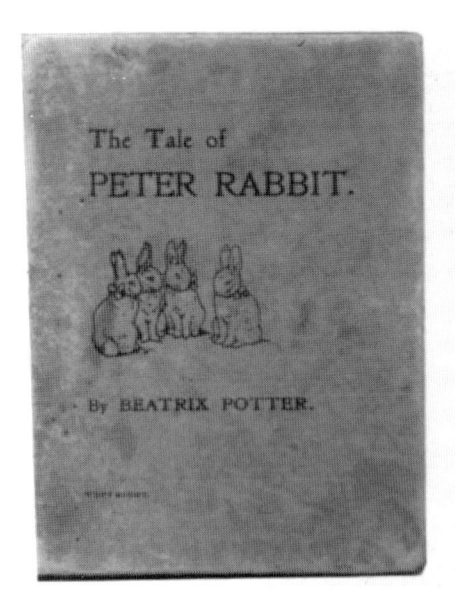

For *The Tale of Peter Rabbit* Beatrix Potter adapted the format of Helen Bannerman's *The Story of Little Black Sambo* (illustration and text facing each other), and The Dumpy Books' small size, to her purposes

' "Roots" of the Peter Rabbit Tales', where Beatrix said that she wanted to publish Peter but was unable to 'find any publisher who agreed with me'. We should take that statement literally: the letter to Marjorie chronicles argument, but not a return 'with or without thanks'. The editor's insistence on a bigger book, the request for poetry, the female staff and the tolerance of argument all suggest to me that she took the book to Nister and was offered an appearance in a holiday annual – but that is just a hunch. What is important is that Beatrix's dealings with editors had been conditioned by Grub Street; and, as the text and picture in Marjorie's letter show, she was considering the tactic that had compelled Nister to give her her price on 'A Frog he would a-fishing go' – withdrawal. And she did withdraw it. On 24 April, she wrote to Marjorie's sister Freda (Frida): 'Miss Potter is sitting upon her book at present & considering! The publisher cannot tell what has become of it.' The accompanying picture portrays Beatrix sitting on a book while a publisher waves his hands in frustration.[13] But this time, the publisher did not give in – and all the publishers to whom she sent the manuscript over the next year declined it.

Considering this situation, it is important to remember that there is a very fine distinction between a work that is original and a work that is unmarketable.

The Tale of Peter Rabbit, as it began its travels, straddled that line. Beatrix was consciously offering a little picture book of a new school. But Peter's story was generically unfamiliar – not poetry, not a sentimental animal tale, not a cartoon-like fantasy, not an awful warning – and its forward-looking nature was obscured by the pacing problems at the end. More crucially, Beatrix's pictures were 'outline illustrations'; and in 1901, black-and-white illustration was still heavily influenced by Morris and Beardsley. She was presenting an altogether different style, but Bannerman's and the Uptons' successes ensured that the future of stylistically innovative picture books lay with color illustration; and a three-color half-tone process was just becoming available. A busy editor besieged by manuscripts and conditioned to read for weaknesses could find many reasons for laying *The Tale of Peter Rabbit* aside.

Rightly believing in her tale's originality, but not aware of the reasons for its difficulties, Beatrix decided to print the book herself. I suspect that it was not until September 1901, upon hearing that she was doing so, that her friend Canon Rawnsley helped her, perhaps tempted by her report that the only editor who had seriously considered it had 'wanted poetry'. Fortunately, when he sent his dreadful rhyming version to Frederick Warne and Co., he included

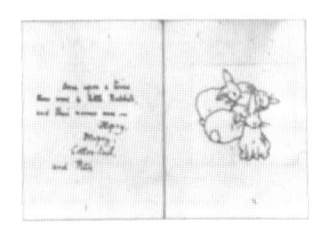

Influenced by the fashion for Morris and Beardsley, Robert Anning Bell's romantic illustration, 'Briar Rose', in *Grimm's Household Tales*, J.M. Dent, 1901, shows one reason why publishers rejected Beatrix Potter's manuscript for *The Tale of Peter Rabbit*

Beatrix's drawings, half her original manuscript, and the news that blocks existed from a forthcoming private printing.

The ensuing exchange is illuminating. Warne wrote to Rawnsley, asking for the rest of Beatrix's manuscript and inquiring, among other things, why all the pictures were not colored. Rawnsley unwisely allowed Beatrix to answer the letter herself, and her tone was one schooled by Grub Street. Instead of offering to color the pictures, or something of that sort, she closed her letter with an abrupt explanation:

> I did not colour the whole book for two reasons – the great expense of good colour printing – and also the rather uninteresting colour of a good many of the subjects which are most of them rabbit-brown and green.[14]

This abruptness almost ended the chances of the publication of *The Tale of Peter Rabbit* for the second time. Writing back to Rawnsley, Warne expressed disappointment with the end of the story and added:

> ... we are persuaded that to make the book a success, it is absolutely necessary that the pictures should be coloured throughout. Miss Potter seems to think the colour would be uninteresting, so that as we differ so materially on this point ... we think it best to decline your kind offer, at any rate this year.[15]

But they left the door open; the manuscript had been carefully edited to produce a book with thirty-two pictures, and the letter insisted that 'each of these should be produced in colour'. This was not a Grub Street ultimatum: it was a negotiation which, while based on a knowledge of the market, treated the author's ideas with respect, considered the book itself in artistic terms and expressed both genuine hesitation and genuine interest. One reason for that interest is embedded in the polite rejection of Rawnsley's poetic version: 'we think there is a great deal to be said for the simple narration; which has been very effectively used in a little book produced last year entitled "Little Black Sambo", though there are many good ideas in your verses which might be introduced with advantage.' Warne wanted a little book to compete with *The Story of Little Black Sambo*. But that could materialize only if Miss Potter could be brought to revise.

Warne's tactful letter brought out the side of Beatrix Potter that respected professional dealing, truthful speaking and genuine knowledge, and the clear hesitation broke down her tendency to resist suggestion and made her rethink her work. In a letter unfortunately lost, she expressed her willingness to revise and sent a few colored pictures for Warne's approval. Having studied them, one of the press's newly successful illustrators, L. Leslie Brooke, told Warne to publish the book, for it would be a success.[16] The assurance coincided with the appearance in October 1901 of Helen Bannerman's second little book, *The Story of Little Black Mingo*, to warm reviews; and Warne, now facing the possibility of a series of miniature golliwog books, accepted *The Tale of Peter Rabbit*.

They acted not a moment too soon, for *The Story of Little Black Mingo* and the Bannerman books that followed it yearly were only a few of the little picture books that appeared in Sambo's wake. Among these, of course, were The Dumpy Books, which Richards published in increasing numbers each year, but other series quickly followed. In 1901, J. M. Dent led the way with The Bairn Books. In 1902, the year *The Tale of Peter Rabbit* was published, Swan Sonnenschein began the Oogley Oo Books, imitating both the format and 'crossover' tone of the early Dumpy Books; and Hodder and Stoughton brought out The Little One's Library, among them *The Story of a Little Coloured Coon*, obviously inspired by *The Story of Little Black Sambo*. Grub Street joined them: Nister brought out The Rosebud Series and Raphael Tuck started The Children's Gem Library, each with a Nesbit story to give it respectability. Thus, in the first year of its publication, *The Tale of Peter Rabbit* was competing with six series of little books. Its performance was all a press (and an author) could wish: 28,000 copies were printed in the last three months of 1902, 7,000 more than *The Story of Little Black Sambo* had sold in a year; 16,500 more copies were printed in 1903.[17]

A vogue for small books. *The Story of Little Black Mingo* (*top left*), two books from Swan Sonnenschein's the Oogley Oo Books (*top right and bottom left*) and one of Dent's The Bairn Books (*bottom right*)

And that, as Beatrix Potter would say, is the story of Peter Rabbit. But there is an epilogue. Forty-one years after the publication of *The Tale of Peter Rabbit*, Janet Adam Smith published what can only be called an encomium on the little books in *The Listener*, remarking that Beatrix's illustrations had behind them the same sense of place as those of Samuel Palmer, Edward Calvert and other English pastoral artists. She sent a copy to Beatrix Potter and received a gruff answer that, while thanking her, wondered at her knowing 'a deal more about the inception of the Peter Rabbit books than I do!' The unkind remark was completely unwarranted by the article; so was the obvious assumption that Smith had accused Beatrix of deriving her style from other painters. Clearly, Smith had conjured up a demon – and the demon appears in Beatrix's letter: 'When first published another outraged authoress (and her publisher) said they were a crib of a horrid little book called "Little Black Sambo". Now you say they are founded on the work of the Immortals . . ..'[18] Five days later, in a letter to Arthur Stephens at Warne, Beatrix mentioned the demon again:

> You may not remember – as regards "Peter Rabbit" – a Mrs Bannerman & her publishers Grant Richards said Peter was imitated from their Dumpy book series and they were rather nasty about it. As a matter of fact, Peter was spontaneously written before "Little Black Sambo" was published.[19]

One would like to know, of course, what happened – particularly because the story is so perplexing. Far from being united co-producers of 'their Dumpy book series' at the time *The Tale of Peter Rabbit* was published, Bannerman and Richards were barely on speaking terms. Despite Bannerman's repeated pleas, Richards had refused to restore the copyright in *The Story of Little Black Sambo* to her, even without remuneration. She thus published *The Story of Little Black Mingo* and all her subsequent books with James Nisbet & Company, who printed them in a format which, excepting the addition of a picture on the front cover, was identical to that of The Dumpy Books.

Apparently, Richards and Bannerman overcame their mutual ill-will, and their 'nastiness' to Beatrix Potter almost certainly did not involve legal action. Neither the Bannerman nor the Potter biographers have found a trace of such action in the archives, and Beatrix's phrase to Stephens 'you may not remember' suggests there was nothing to look for. And there was no case: *The Tale of Peter Rabbit* was indeed written before *The Story of Little Black Sambo*, and if the latter was derivative, *The Story of Little Black Mingo*, which featured a mugger and an egg-eating mongoose right out of Kipling, was worse. Nor could Richards, who published *The Story of Little Yellow Yang-Lo* in 1903, take a moral high ground.

What seems possible, given the size of the vogue for small books, is that Richards (perhaps with Bannerman's permission) wrote a piece in the *Publisher's Circular*, or one of the reviews, decrying the number of books on the 1902 Christmas market that were, in Beatrix's elegant phrase, 'a crib' from *The Story of Little Black Sambo*. For this, there was ample justification: the Oogley Oo Books were clearly Dumpy clones, and *The Story of a Little Coloured Coon* came close to outright plagiarism. *The Tale of Peter Rabbit* could easily have been included in the piece simply because it was a book of the same type and size – or perhaps because it was *The Story of Little Black Sambo*'s only real competitor.

But whatever happened, it questioned Beatrix's originality just as she was beginning her career. And, as I have tried to show, while her artwork and story were unimpeachably her own, she had consciously adopted Bannerman's format. It was, after all, a good idea – one whose possibilities she increasingly realized by giving her stories a local habitation and a name. But it was perhaps the knowledge that she *had* used Bannerman's format that made the nastiness hurt. And it was perhaps that pain that made her so defensive about the little books. That defensiveness is there in ' "Roots" of the Peter Rabbit Tales' – which, incidentally, it took *four years* for Bertha Mahony to persuade her to write. The story of Peter's beginnings is backed up not only by the post-Romantic portrait of the artist, but by the assurance that 'Noel has the letter yet' – an assertion that appears also in the 1925 letter to Anne Carroll Moore. The defensiveness lingers in the unnecessary assurance to Stephens that 'Peter was spontaneously written', and thus, by implication, a great home story like *Alice's Adventures in Wonderland*, *The Jungle Book*, *Just So Stories*, *Peter Pan*, and *The Wind in the Willows*.

I do not for a minute doubt that, or accuse Beatrix Potter of anything but a solid business sense. As Peter Hollindale has said, 'a large part of any book is written not by its author but by the world its author lives in'.[20] *The Tale of Peter Rabbit* was a book of its time. If a competitive spirit led Beatrix Potter to use a fashionable format, if the guidance and tact of an editor encouraged her to draw and redraw, think and rethink, experiment and have confidence in her genius, that in no way lessens the achievement of her work. Her patience, her talent, her willingness to learn bore fruit in a book not just of its time, but of our time, and of time to come.

1 Morse, Jane Crowell (ed.), *Beatrix Potter's Americans: Selected Letters*, Boston, MA: The Horn Book, 1982, p. 192
2 Hollindale, Peter, 'Beatrix Potter and Natural History', *Working on the Beatrix Potter Jigsaw*, Beatrix Potter Studies IX, The Beatrix Potter Society, 2001, p. 62
3 Richards, Grant, *Author Hunting, by an Old Literary Sportsman: Memories of Years Spent Mainly in Publishing, 1897–1925*, London: Hamish Hamilton, 1934, pp. 30–1
4 Stetz, Margaret D. and Lasner, Mark Samuels, *In the 1890s: Literary Publishing at the Bodley Head*, Washington, DC: Georgetown University Press, 1990, p. viii
5 Linder, Leslie (ed.), *The Journal of Beatrix Potter*, London: Frederick Warne, new edition 1989, pp. 13–14

6   Briggs, Julia, *A Woman of Passion: The Life of E. Nesbit 1858–1924*, New York: New Amsterdam Books, 1987, p. 122
7   Watling, Roy, 'Mischievous mushrooms: Beatrix Potter's affair with fungi – facts and misunderstandings', *Working on the Beatrix Potter Jigsaw*, Beatrix Potter Studies IX, The Beatrix Potter Society, 2001, p. 76
8   Taylor, Judy (ed.), *Letters to Children from Beatrix Potter*, London: Frederick Warne, 1992, p. 100
9   Richards, op. cit., p. 33
10 Hay, Edith, *Sambo Sahib: The Story of Little Black Sambo and Helen Bannerman*, Edinburgh: Paul Harris Publishing, 1981, pp. 25–8
11 'More about Little Black Sambo', *Signal: Approaches to Children's Books*, Issue 91, January 2000, p. 64
12 Taylor, op. cit., p 66
13 Ibid., p. 70
14 Taylor, Judy (ed.), *Beatrix Potter's Letters*, London: Frederick Warne, 1989, p. 55
15 Unpublished letter from Frederick Warne & Co. to Rev. Canon Rawnsley, 11 September 1901, Warne Archive
16 Brooke, Henry, *Leslie Brooke and Johnny Crow*, London: Frederick Warne, 1982, pp. 36–7
17 Taylor, Judy, *That Naughty Rabbit: Beatrix Potter and Peter Rabbit*, London: Frederick Warne, new edition, 2002, pp. 49, 51
18 Taylor, *Beatrix Potter's Letters*, op. cit., p. 454
19 Ibid., p. 455
20 'Ideology and the Children's Book', *Signal: Approaches to Children's Books*, Issue 55, January 1988, p. 15

The Typographic Adventures of The Tale of Peter Rabbit

DOUGLAS MARTIN

A PRELIMINARY explanation of the typographer or book designer's work may be helpful. The book designer stands in the same relationship to publisher and printer as the architect does to his client and to the builder. Joseph Moxon (*Mechanick Exercises*, 1683–4) writes that by a 'Typographer' he does not mean a 'Printer' but 'such a one, who by his own Judgement, from solid reasoning with himself, can either perform, or direct others to perform from the beginning to the end, all the Handy-works and Physical operations relating to *Typographie*.'

To make that definition fit today's book typographer, one would have to add the gamut of illustration, photography and picture research; and to assume an extensive knowledge of book culture, the book trades and marketing, and those categories of book with which the typographer is principally concerned – in my own case children's books, academic and reference books, books about music and the arts, and books about books. Many book designers choose to be freelance, working for the multi-nationals but also with individuals, societies and institutions for whom publications are occasional or even unique affairs. So the designer can work from a manuscript – or even an idea – through to a manufactured and marketable product; sometimes with an author or editor, sometimes as part of a large team.

This shaping process starts with fundamental considerations: what market? how many copies? which format? what kind of illustration? And from these follow design choices in relation to the text: typeface; number of pages; paper; hierarchy of headings; treatment of reference apparatus; briefing the illustrator, photographer or picture researcher; obtaining quotes from printers and suppliers; and showing specimen pages to clients. Then drawing up a production schedule; typesetting the text; incorporating illustrations; making up into pages; designing the jacket and binding and so on. Today the computer is the great unifier of this mass of diverse information, rendering obsolete many of the elaborate roughs and calculations, layouts and paste-ups of the recent past; and allowing proofs or disks to be run-off as required for proof-reading, estimating and final platemaking. Thus today's design unit is perforce the typesetter and colour originator as well for many books. A contemporary way to think of book design, perhaps, is as desk top publishing plus the experience of several lifetimes (however rapidly acquired); a meticulous obsession with order, simplicity and getting every detail right; and – above all – undiminishing enthusiasm for the uniqueness of each new manuscript that comes along.

How differently books were planned and produced a century ago! Successive technological advances (the latest and most significant of which are still being assimilated) place higher standards within universal reach. It is a time for great, if not unqualified, optimism.

Our wealth of typefaces to choose from, and the flexibility with which we can set from them, would be the envy of that earlier generation of printers. Affordable colour printing is available wherever it is required. The quality and choice of materials is limited only by economic constraints. Yet bookbinders of the early twentieth century, for example, would be amazed at the drab business we have made of their craft, perhaps through lack of courage and imagination. But there are signs that even this may change as book publishing realigns itself for a new role in society.

Above all, the working relationship between publisher and printer has changed out of recognition since 1902. No book designers in the modern sense were active in trade publishing in Beatrix Potter's day, but touching on our field of children's books there were the precepts of Walter Crane; the lovely volumes crafted by those master colour-woodblock printers restored to history by Ruari McLean; imposing gift books designed for non-children and culminating in Pogány's Wagnerian visions of the total book; as well as the first stirrings of the international avant-garde.

Few ordinary trade books, however, were touched by such aesthetic currents. The general attitude was that as soon as the words seemed right, if not sooner, send them to the printer. So much more was then expected of and left to the printer. Although Beatrix Potter and her publishers were exceptionally clear-sighted about their requirements, the printer would still be expected to work out the typography. He would have to set such short texts as these by hand, for the gradual transition to hot metal for book composition was scarcely under way by 1902.

Of the three- and four-colour letterpress half-tone processes of those days (as of mine), the least said the better. Whereas most printing and printmaking processes – Gutenberg's own method, engraving, autolithography – sprang to life fully armed, it was a failing of the last century to live with dud processes well beyond their day. Photo-mechanical colour reproduction was still in its infancy when Beatrix Potter's drawings were first reproduced, and although offset colour printing advanced considerably during the second half of the century, permitting improvements in that area, the state of *typesetting* lagged behind until very recently and only now, as will be demonstrated, lets us improve more than marginally upon the earliest editions of these books. Certainly I found it a fascinating commission to redesign Beatrix Potter's 'little books', which happened to arrive just as I felt on reasonable terms with the latest wave of technology in the studio. I hope that it may provide an interesting tale.

How clever of Warne to light on a designer who had not met Peter Rabbit before. Each and every design project should set out from a *tabula rasa*, but it is a huge advantage to have no preconceptions, no predispositions, no inherited reverence of the kind that, as one soon came to see, had led to the anonymous perpetuation of slovenliness and error in the past.

From the moment £20,000 worth of the privately-printed edition of *The Tale of Peter Rabbit* was pressed momentarily into my ungloved hands, the rightness – the small miracle even – of this modest format was apparent to me. I am confident there will always be a place for facsimiles of these early editions, but what had happened to the product in the intervening years? Taken together, later editions provide a history of twentieth-century book production in microcosm; a record of changes which occurred during a century of typesetting, colour reproduction, papermaking and bookbinding – the bad alongside the good.

It soon became apparent, for example, how the change to bleak white paper in itself (in the name of fashion or progress, of course) is enough to transform the entire aesthetic and flavour of these little books – it is as though a good home-baked loaf were to be replaced overnight by the sliced, white, supermarket variety! And there is evidence of other such mindless changes.

Not that the first editions were in any sense flawless. The typesetting exhibits stylistic mannerisms typical of the period. Text and plates are poorly positioned, frequently just below the optical centre of the page. The twenty-three titles did not share any common series grid or styling (as would be the norm nowadays). But author, publisher and printer were doing their level best, and their collective sense of purpose won through. Although there were significant gains as improvements in colour reproduction brought us closer to the artist's originals, most reprints were inferior to the originals as printed books. This is largely because the texts and their layout and arrangement on the page were regarded as sacrosanct by later editors and designers, so that fresh typesettings introduced as many eyesores as they eliminated. All adaptations to new manufacturing processes, substitutions of materials, changes for the sake of change or fashion, or statutory innovations (such as bar-codes and imprint copy) stamped each book with the signs of its date of manufacture and frequently obscured the authenticity of the original design.

The initial briefing over an excellent lunch with the team at Warne and subsequent research and discussion enabled the objectives of the redesign to be framed: for *The Tale of Peter Rabbit* our intention was simply to 'reinterpret 1902 intentions with the benefit of our more sophisticated resources a century later'. This would entail a revision of: the editorial and typographic conventions adopted by this visually acute author, her publisher and printer; the typefaces available to them; their format and *mise-en-page*; their approach to binding and jacket materials and design and their choice of text paper. I would like to take a few examples from each of these areas, and apologise in advance for the concentration on minutiae (but what is design if not the sum of countless resolved minutiae?). The merit of the 'little books' is that visual comparisons are readily made and that with so few words to a page the effect of the smallest changes can be instantly spotted. I say this with feeling since the last revision of a long-dormant design to pass through the studio was for *Whitaker's Almanack*!

Warne's senior editor, Diana Syrat, and I set out some initial guidelines for the editorial and typographic conventions we should use, but right up to the last moment found ourselves comparing alternative solutions to problems of detail as they arose. This was an absorbing and altogether pleasurable exercise.

Collins's *Author & Printer* first appeared in 1905, and its present incarnation is as *The Oxford Dictionary for Writers and Editors*. It might be thought that a substitution of the received practice for these respective periods would yield a valid solution, for example the em—dash was used in 1905, but the en–dash is used in 2000. But on the contrary we found our own *via media* worked best on the page: this led us deliberately to preserve and even accentuate the period flavour in places, whilst quietly modernising in others.

As examples of deference to the period, we opted for double quotes rather than the single quotes used in 1902; full points were retained after Mr. and Mrs.; and the designer argued doggedly for the retention of the little word 'BY' on the title-page. We also introduced the single ornament sparingly – perhaps half-a-dozen times in the course of twenty-three titles – to emphasise a break or mark the separation of unrelated material.

The treatment of verse was found to be particularly slapdash, with many unnecessary turnover lines and scant regard for rhythm or scansion. The two nursery rhyme books are extreme cases, where an uncritical editor and an ill-trained compositor made a hash of things, even failing to indicate where one rhyme ended and the next began. Later re-settings slavishly followed the letter rather than the spirit of these primary versions.

Turning to the typeface, *The Tale of Peter Rabbit* was originally set by hand in a nondescript old-style typeface for which the punches would have been pantographically engraved, that is to say, reduced for all sizes from a set of huge and lifeless engineer's drawings. The printer, evidently and typically, possessed neither the sizes of type nor the skill to fit the opening initials properly; a detail in which all subsequent typesetters have scrupulously followed his lead. In truth there was little that Beatrix Potter or her publisher could have done to obtain a better standard from the trade at the time. They had gone to the best colour printer of the day for their purpose, but as Ruari McLean has written:

> Edmund Evans was born in Southwark in 1826, two years before Thomas Bewick's death; he lived to be the last of the great commercial wood-engravers, and the best known, through the children's books which made his name a household world. When he died in 1905, the days of the commercial wood-engraving firms were over; books, magazines, and newspapers were illustrated with photographically prepared and chemically etched zinc process blocks.[1]

Early on in the design process, the designer has to take a cluster of almost simultaneous decisions on inter-related matters – format, typeface and the look of the reading page. If these decisions are made rightly, then everything else down to the tiniest refinement of detail should fall into place, and the resultant book will be sound and pleasing. There was no question of changing *The Tale of Peter Rabbit*'s format – no one wanted to do that for a moment – so attention focused on selecting the very best typeface for the job.

There are literally thousands of typefaces (or 'fonts' as we are now supposed to call them) available for digital setting, and yet my shortlist came down to just two, Caslon and Baskerville, with a decided preference for the former. The story does not end there, for there are more versions of each in the catalogues than of Beethoven's Fifth on record. I would like to try to explain why the Founder's Caslon from H. W. Caslon & Company Limited is so special.

Before the work of William Caslon I, 1693–1766, no types of any distinction had been manufactured in Britain. Our printers from Caxton onwards worked with types imported from the Continent, latterly from Holland. Caslon's types share the best qualities to be found in British rural architecture, interiors, furniture and craftsmanship of the mid-eighteenth century, although it is to John Baskerville, 1705–75, a man attuned to the changes in printing and papermaking brought about by the industrial revolution as well as to the neo-classical tastes of the Adam brothers and Wedgwood, that we must look for a more urbane and progressive contribution.

Caslon's types deserve to be regarded as a national treasure. The American historian D. B. Updike's shrewd evaluation of them (dating from 1922) is worth quoting at length:

> Why are William Caslon's types so excellent and so famous? To explain this and make it really clear, is difficult. While he modelled his letters on Dutch types, they were much better; for he introduced into his fonts a quality of interest, a variety of design, and a delicacy of modelling, which few Dutch types possessed. Dutch fonts were monotonous, but Caslon's fonts were not so. His letters when analysed, especially in the smaller sizes, are not perfect individually, but in mass their effect is agreeable. That is, I think, their secret – a perfection of the whole, derived from harmonious but not necessarily perfect individual letter-forms. To say precisely how Caslon arrived at his effects is not simple; but he did so because he was an artist. He knew how to make types, if ever a man did, that were . . . 'friendly to the eye', or 'comfortable'. . . . Furthermore, his types are thoroughly English. There are other letters more elegant; for the Caslon characters do not compare in that respect with the letters of Garamond or Grandjean. But in their defects and qualities they are the result of a taste typically Anglo-Saxon, and represent to us the flowering of a sturdy English tradition in typography. . . . Caslon types are, too, so beautiful in mass, and above all so legible and 'common-sense', that they can never be disregarded, and I doubt if they will ever be displaced.[2]

Until very recently, despite the multitude of fonts that bore Caslon's name, there was no version that I would have readily chosen to use, and would probably have pursued the alternative, Baskerville, line of enquiry. But then Founder's Caslon was made available by the International Typeface Corporation. This proved to be a true facsimile of Caslon's original types in his 12pt, 30pt and 42pt sizes only, and I was delighted with the trial settings made for *The Tale of Peter Rabbit*.

I contacted the designer and printing historian, Justin Howes, who was behind this venture, and found that he was working on and planning to issue for the computer the entire Caslon Old Face repertoire in facsimile himself (as ITC had withdrawn from so ambitious an undertaking). All fourteen sizes have now appeared (and may be studied or purchased on the internet at www.hwcaslon.com), thus making available to the book designer all Caslon's characters for each and every size which, it should be stressed, were originally engraved by hand, and thus the design underwent constant variation and adaptation according to the optical desiderata for each individual size. Hence its life and sparkle in comparison to the general run of metal, film or digital type designs of the past century and more, for which all sizes have been generated from a single set, or at best two or three sets, of master drawings. Founder's Caslon is something of a first for digital typography, and thanks to Justin Howes's generosity in making available pre-publication fonts, the centenary edition of the 'little books' are the first to be set in it.

In the design of books of all kinds there is a functional, or ergonomic, relationship between format, the size and shape of the book, and type-size. At the heart of this is line-length. For continuous reading, and well-spaced type-setting, the optimum line-length will be found – depending on many other factors – to be somewhere between ten and thirteen average words to the line. But in the case of the original Beatrix Potter settings this average is as low as six words to the line. And these lines are justified or 'squared up' on the right-hand side!

Inevitably the quality of the setting suffers, and wide 'rivers' run down the page as the space between words exceeds the interlinear space. This matters because the unsightliness which is apparent when the typesetting is *viewed* purely as Gestalt – as an abstract pattern of black on white – is an outward sign of the real turmoil and confusion caused by the attempt to *read* such typesetting. Although the number of actual words to a page is not many, in places we are brought close to the point at which the mechanics of reading break down. (Put another way, if we picked up and tried to read a paperback novel set with this degree of excessive word spacing, then we would lay it aside after no more than a paragraph or two – probably blaming the author or our own tiredness for this typographic 'power-cut'.)

So it was immediately obvious to me that the original and later typesettings were all flawed in this fundamental way, and the real challenge was to improve this situation without throwing the baby out with the bath water,

THE squirrels followed and listened. The first little bird flew into the bush where Timmy and Goody Tiptoes were quietly tying up their bags, and it sang—"'Who's-bin digging-up *my* nuts? Who's been digging-up *my*-nuts?"

Timmy Tiptoes went on with his work without replying; indeed, the little bird did not expect an answer. It was only singing its natural song, and it meant nothing at all.

'Rivers', or where the eye takes the line of least resistance that is, without losing sight of the special character and identity of the original books. In order to reach the best solution, I tried to reconstruct how this situation might have arisen in the first place. This process brought a deeper appreciation of the creative achievement these books represent and some insight into the secret of their continuing success. To my own satisfaction, at least, I unravelled the sequence of underlying *right* decisions that preceded this *impasse* for which there was no practical printer's solution at that time.

The first decision to applaud was the choice of 140×105 mm ($5\frac{1}{2}$ inches by 4 inches) as the format for these books. If you had to find a size that the very young child has to take in *both* hands in order to turn the pages and discover what happens then you could hardly do better. The mini versions of new and established picture books, such as *The Very Hungry Caterpillar* and Wildsmith's and Piénkowski's respective *Christmas* stories – that have been such a feature of the past fifteen years or so – have only re-invented the wheel in this respect.

Now let us choose the best size of type for early reading over a fair age-range in terms of ability, which will also be fine for the adult storyteller to read whilst 'sharing' the book, probably in subdued lighting. Again, today's typographer would endorse the size chosen, unsurprisingly, since typographic verities do not change, only educationalists' perceptions of them.

Bring these two decisions together with the artwork and a *text-panel* suggests itself as a result of balancing type and illustration as they face each other on the spread. Of course it is all there instinctively in the manuscripts and sketches – knowing how many words should appear on a quiet page and how many on a busy one. The average line length of six words which results also accords with the aims of simplicity and accessibility for children who, having previously been read to, take up the exciting task of reading for themselves.

The serious spacing problem which creeps in at this point is a product of the rigidity of the typesetting systems of the day, and indeed of all those which prevailed or succeeded one another right up until the 1980s. Justified typesetting to a fixed but narrow measure results in wretchedly gappy word spacing as we have seen. The compositor was induced to break many words to minimize this effect, and the tedious process of setting type line by line – not unlike knitting – largely precluded going back to improve on lines already completed.

But nowadays typesetting is at the designer's fingertips. The cost of setting has fallen to about ten per cent of what it was for most of the twentieth century in real terms. The speed, flexibility and precision of QuarkXPress on the Mac is breathtaking, particularly for one who has worked through four decades to the irksome limitations of one hot-metal, photosetting and digital system after another.

> THEN he tried to find his way straight across the garden, but he became more and more puzzled. Presently, he came to a pond where Mr. McGregor filled his water-cans. A white cat was staring at some gold-fish; she sat very, very still, but now and then the tip of her tail twitched as if it were alive. Peter thought it best to go away without speaking to her; he had heard about cats from his cousin, little Benjamin Bunny.

Typesetting of 1902 to a fixed measure or line length, with the inevitable gappy spacing (*left*), and the typesetting solution adopted for 2002 (*right*)

What then was to be done? Modern practice would be to set with a fixed close word space and leave the right-hand edge ragged or unjustified. I tried this and was astonished at how strongly this procedure, which is almost the norm for picture books nowadays, violated the Beatrix Potter idiom. Her drawings are all either bounded by rectangular frames or take the form of symmetrical vignettes, and demand a static rectangular block on the facing page. Asymmetrical typography changes the whole dynamic, and destroys the restfulness of those double-page spreads on which her self-contained world quietly unfolds. It further struck me that, although ragged setting has appeared sporadically over the centuries in all sorts of odd places, it would have been an anachronism to impose it in the context of a narrative, however straight-forward, dating from 1902. Although few people could be consciously aware of this historical transgression, the incongruity seemed as great as if children of that age had been redrawn wearing reversed baseball caps! However, an alternative using ragged setting was submitted without comment to the team at Warne, who were unanimous in throwing it out.

Reviewing all the factors which singly or in combination might ameliorate the situation, my attention was caught by one not normally considered as a variable, yet which turned out to yield the best answer: the line-length or

A rejected proposal: lines set ragged or unjustified (*left*). The 2002 adopted proposal: lines set squared-up or justified – in period (*right*)

'measure' itself. Since Gutenberg's day, one of the first things an apprentice compositor has been taught is to set a fixed measure in the composing stick; for any deviation from this standard will lead to dire consequences later on in the printing process. So the sanctity of the fixed measure still retains the force of a taboo.

But in the special case of the Beatrix Potter books, we have a situation where the sizes and shapes of the illustrations vary from spread to spread, and so I came up with the notion of having a fluctuating measure. 'Type is not made of india-rubber', the typographer soon learns, but to stretch the measure in and out like a rubber-band within carefully judged parameters certainly produces effects that make one question that maxim.

Typically, there are as many as twenty or thirty variations for the word arrangement within a typical page of text. Reviewing these alternatives time and time again, one or two will be found to have almost ideal spacing, and it may actually be possible to use one of the results of this 'first filtering' as it may be called. But to introduce one of a whole list of possible refinements at a given point in the page and repeat the whole process yields a fresh set with variant word and line arrangements below the point at which the change was introduced.

In this way, by following a series of carefully drawn-up rules (ensuring, for instance, that the measure on facing pages must always be identical) a visually acceptable standard of typesetting can be obtained in these tricky circumstances. In fact, the method proved so successful that the editor was able to veto the majority of the remaining word-breaks, so that very few occur throughout the twenty-three titles.

Incidentally, such close attention to the resetting, character by character and line by line, also constitutes a form of bibliographical analysis. Over the two decades separating the first title from the last there were clearly changes in editorial staff and styles at Warne, and variations in the levels of skill and attention brought to the task are evident. *The Tale of Peter Rabbit* itself – where, as one would expect, top-level scrutiny of the proofs attended to every detail – and one or two other titles are head and shoulders above the rest in these respects. It is equally apparent that there were no grids or layouts for this series, but then it would be exceptional to find any at the dates in question, and so the *mise-en-page* was left to the printer's make-up and makeshift optical judgements. No later reprints tackled the problem of arbitrary positioning on the page, or attempted to treat the preliminary pages as being in series, let alone place all twenty-three titles on a grid as we have done, so that margins are harmonious throughout and details such as pagination are standardised.

The series 'just grew' in the first place. No one could have foretold how many titles there would eventually be. The texture of the tales developed from an initial sequence of picture-book episodes (*The Tale of Peter Rabbit*) to continuous narrative (*The Tailor of Gloucester*), to a short novel in chapters (*The Tale of Little Pig Robinson*), to minimal picture-book captions (*The Story of Miss Moppet*) and to verse form (*Cecily Parsley's Nursery Rhymes* and *Appley Dapply's Nursery Rhymes*).

Thus the original typography had to be improvised to cope with each new set of requirements as it arose. But our brief was to take an 'overview' – the first there had ever been. Thus we could observe, for example, that the large initial with which each page of text in *The Tale of Peter Rabbit* opened, does not work nearly so well for *The Story of Miss Moppet*, where there are far fewer words to a page, and that it actually obstructed reading continuity where a simple rhyme has to be split-up over consecutive spreads. And so choices between the alternatives submitted by the designer were all taken with an eye to the series as a whole, as well as to the title under consideration. We opted to use a large fitted initial for the opening page of each story or section, and a small capital opening for each succeeding page.

For many text pages there would be more than one viable solution – possibly the spacing could be greatly improved by letting a reasonable word-break through – and so all these alternatives would be proofed and submitted for an editorial decision. When it came to the styling of title-pages, dedications, initials and so forth, more variants were submitted and more people took part in the decision-making. The designer does not fear such a democratic process: either he subtly loads the dice, or accepts the verdict of professional colleagues that he has not made his case convincingly enough. The final choice for the series title-page, for example, lay between two versions. I felt that both were reasonable typographic solutions, but was not surprised that the preferred version proved to be the one which uses the period Beatrix Potter capitals.

The use of the Beatrix Potter alphabet here led on naturally to the treatment of the jackets and case bindings, for which it supplies the brand name identity. And so it was good to have set up a link between the lettering of the title inside the book and on the covers. This Beatrix Potter lettering was redrawn, following the best of the hand-drawn titling for the original editions, as part of the 1985 exercise to standardise jackets, and it has now been digitised for use as a (protected) typographic font.

There are drawbacks to any typeface which sets out to copy freehand lettering or calligraphy. Individual letter forms may be faithfully reproduced, but such types cannot hope to incorporate the skills by which the scribe varies these forms and fits them together into specific words. The spacing will always

F. WARNE & Co Beatrix Potter's

PETER RABBIT TYPE
ABCDEFGHIJKLMNOPQRS
TUVWXYZ
&ÆT RR O⁰ ⓒ ⓡ "" – " – .;?

'Beatrix Potter' type: a digital font derived from the lettering style for early bindings and jackets look awkward and irregular compared to the 'real thing', and the designer using such types for book jacket designs simply cannot use them 'off the peg'. Some manipulation of the characters themselves and the spaces between them is necessary, and whereas in the past metal characters had to be filed down for closer fitting or spaced out with strips of brass and paper, or camera-copy had to be endlessly cut and pasted, the computer makes this relatively painless. But the effort was always repaid.

The credit for jacket and binding design should go to Ronnie Fairweather, who had been working in-house at Warne on the problem for a long time before I became involved with the project. Such a redesign is a major marketing undertaking these days, involving consultation with partners responsible for promoting sales around the world.

Apparently so many of those consulted in the marketing research process considered the inclusion of an *ex libris* on the front endpaper to be such a vital ingredient that the fate of the scrollwork borders drawn by Beatrix Potter and incorporating characters from the books was sealed. Ronnie Fairweather's new design with the characters subliminally present in a lighter shade of blue is a valid re-interpretation, and functions more as endpapers should: one eighteenth-century German writer describes them as 'theatre curtains – they rise and the play begins'.

To explain what became of the original endpapers, I would like to quote from the new edition of Judy Taylor's *That Naughty Rabbit*:

> In order not to lose the well-known full-colour endpapers altogether, Frederick Warne selected Beatrix Potter's design of book characters to use as a half-title, or introductory page, for the new editions, the pictures acting as a frame for the book title. The version that now appears in *The Tale of Peter Rabbit* is the one she first drew for *Squirrel Nutkin*, showing characters from the three books that had been published to date, together with the tea-set from *The Tailor of Gloucester* and Mrs McGregor's pie from *The Tale of Peter Rabbit*. Beatrix Potter went on to adapt the design to incorporate other characters and these variations have been included in later titles in the series so that the interested reader can now find all six of her endpaper designs among the centenary editions.[3]

The success of the new binding ensemble owes much to Warne's choice of a greyed cornflower-blue background for the series. This softer colour is much kinder to the illustrations, and makes the titling on the front board less assertive. The idea is that the jacket has already done any necessary selling, and the binding is just an extra revealed only to the especially curious or destructive child (or so runs the theory that justifies making no particular effort over binding design). The binding design for the normal edition had to remain a basic one in paper, so that the *de luxe* editions which will be called for from time to time may really go to town with cloth, gilt edges, headbanding, markers, and the authentic hand-pasted labels! For the moment spot-varnishing substitutes effectively for pasted-on labels.

It was fundamental that the jacket design should not change to the extent that the integrity of the product was questioned – the concept of 'gradualism' in the evolution of logos and packaging. In other words no one should consciously spot any difference. But we are confident that framing the spot drawings not merely echoes the binding labels but has the desired effect of drawing the eye towards the picture and to the book. Moving the type away from the edges and towards the picture also helps in this. Does it make sense if I suggest that with the jacket design that went before, the eye tended to bounce off the surface with the reaction 'too much white'?

For many years now the besetting sin of the papers used in picture-books has been that they have been too *white* – of a nasty blueish high-white quality redolent of strip lighting and washing powder commercials – and too *glossy*, shiny and reflective. Our paper prescription was straightforward. We sought a matt, ivory-toned quality that would bulk adequately, without feeling too stiff as the pages were turned. There would be no opacity problem with such a paper.

Jacket design for the 1987 edition (*left*) and the 2002 design (*right*)

Only towards the close of a design project that took up several months of my life (in this case the greater part of the first half of 2001) does the degree of attachment, affection even, formed towards the subject sink in, and yet the files must be cleared to make room for incoming briefs. All the time I was actually working with these texts and these drawings, I tried to see them as products of their own time and place, within my experience of projects with a historical dimension. But a sense of this author and artist 'looking over my shoulder' became increasingly and disconcertingly real: to the extent that Beatrix Potter now takes up her position with me in the company of those contemporary creators of picture books that I have sometimes been privileged to work with. If pressed I would instance Janet and Allan Ahlberg in the 1980s. For with such rare authors, the end is not finished words and pictures alone, but a vision of the manufactured book. Beatrix Potter was similarly obsessed with preserving the freshness and spontaneity of her invention; understanding, intervening and turning to advantage the materials and production processes at hand; and somehow planning for the future of her books as they encounter new generations of readers.

1 McLean, Ruari (ed.), *The Reminiscences of Edmund Evans: wood-engraver & colour printer 1826–1905*, Oxford: The Clarendon Press, 1967, p. vii
2 Updike, D.B., *Printing Types: Their History, Forms and Use*, Cambridge MA: Harvard University Press, second edition, 1937, pp. 105–6
3 Taylor, Judy, *That Naughty Rabbit*, London: Frederick Warne, new edition, 2002, pp. 101–2

The Frederick Warne Archive and Beatrix Potter

ELIZABETH BOOTH

WHEN THE BEATRIX Potter Society invited me to give a talk at their Conference, I had to think very carefully about my subject. Beatrix Potter has, apparently, been 'done to death'. Every shop you see, from Waterstone's in Charing Cross Road to Airport Gifts in Anchorage, boasts a stunning display of Peter Rabbit. There are a substantial number of books about Beatrix Potter, from the straightforward biographical and literary to the less commercial and more scholarly studies published by the Society. Possible angles on Beatrix Potter seem to be endless, even though many of the more obvious themes have already been covered. Where could I find that informative, unique approach that such a knowledgeable group as the Society might find entertaining and useful?

In exploring the various Beatrix Potter collections for possible clues, I realised that my subject was staring me in the face. At the Warne office on the Strand two substantial rooms are filled with archive material about Beatrix Potter, and the digital archive that I began to develop almost ten years ago carries records of over 9,000 images, objects and manuscripts, with cataloguing work still continuing today. There are sketchbooks, schoolbooks, letters, journals and photographs, all lovingly preserved from day two, if not day one, of her life. It is almost as if someone, somewhere, knew that Beatrix Potter, more than 130 years after her birth, would become the subject of constant curiosity, investigation and professional questioning.

The Potter collections that make up the database were being carefully collated even during her lifetime and they continue to be lovingly cared for today. Despite their scale, they remain incomplete and one of the most intriguing aspects of working with them is trying to understand how new discoveries – new works of art or letters, or simply a new fact about an 'old friend' – can cast new light and perspectives on the Beatrix Potter story and the collections. Finding a photograph of Beatrix's uncle, Sir Henry Roscoe, with his old pal Mr Bunsen, throws an interesting light on her family connections and also on the inspiration for her drawing 'A Dream of Toasted Cheese', for example! The different relationships and links that must be highlighted in the collection underline the need for archiving work to be sensitive, flexible and ongoing. Everything we do in this respect is only building on earlier work.

The research carried out by Leslie Linder, Judy Taylor, Anne Hobbs and Irene Whalley has provided critical signposts to give structure and context to future research, as well as coherent stories to engage the public and to stimulate further interest, and their books will continue to provide the core texts about the work and life of Beatrix Potter. Linder's work in first collecting and then cataloguing Beatrix Potter memorabilia provides the backbone of the resource, and the collections we have today would be less well understood had he not taken the trouble to document at such an early stage. Judy Taylor's work in recording the letters of Beatrix Potter, and her research for the biography *Beatrix Potter: Artist, Storyteller and Countrywoman*, have provided much of the essential material so important to the collections, and her writing gives the authoritative view of Beatrix, serving as a benchmark for all new research about her.

The central point around which all this activity revolves is Frederick Warne & Co. They have a wonderful collection of their own to care for, and they have provided the impetus – and funding – for the development of the database that records and provides access to so much of the collection's material about Beatrix Potter. Warne came into Beatrix Potter's life in 1901 when they were preparing for the publication of *The Tale of Peter Rabbit*, and they have been her publishers ever since. She left the copyright in her work to them on her death in 1943 and since then they have continued to develop the publishing and merchandising programme which she began.

The Frederick Warne Archive, a collection that I have been responsible for managing for the past ten years, is their own heritage collection of Beatrix Potter, and charts her close relationship with them and her in-depth involvement in every aspect of the publication and promotion of her books. As a corporate archive it can offer only limited access to scholarly researchers; however, Warne have contributed to many exhibition projects, and they will continue to do what they can to bring the collection to the public.

The Archive includes the twenty-eight original illustrations for *The Tale of Peter Rabbit*, as well as hundreds of other works of art, thousands of letters, manuscripts, editions of the 'little books' and samples of the early merchandise. The letters really sit at the core of the collection and provide the backbone by which we can link, research and give significance to other items. For example, the rubber toys of Peter Rabbit might appear to be somewhat inconsequential – until you find the letters which Beatrix wrote about them and realise that they reveal valuable things about her as a businesswoman and entrepreneur, as well as providing an interesting historical point on the development of the merchandise. There are over one thousand handwritten letters from Beatrix Potter to Warne in the collection – principally business letters, but also some personal ones.

In addition to the Frederick Warne Archive of original material, they hold a photographic record of almost every Beatrix Potter item held in the British national collections, as well as some in private hands, and this forms the basis of what we call quite simply 'the database', which contains more than 9,000 images. That is more than 9,000 photographs, letters, drawings and articles of memorabilia, all somehow connected with Beatrix Potter and all providing material evidence of her life. It is particularly illuminating to be able to research all this material together in one repository, as so many items work together to give 'added value' to others. For example, the book art held principally by the National Trust can act as a valuable magnet to museum visitors hungry for all things to do with Peter Rabbit. Then, through a complementary display of 'background art', perhaps chosen from the Victoria and Albert Museum, we can begin to tell the story of Beatrix Potter's skill as an artist and naturalist, thus introducing new themes to a wider audience. At the other end of the spectrum, serious research into Beatrix Potter is facilitated by being able to cross-reference and check images, letters and artefacts side by side. Items grow in meaning when associated with other items.

The depth of the Beatrix Potter resource is something that can encourage open thinking about her and it has enabled us to get to the point of our understanding of her as a person thus far. However, there is one disadvantage of having too much information available, and that is that it can be difficult to know where to look for the right link. I feel that part of the role of archivists and curators is to try to shape meaningful research tools in order to help researchers not only to find the immediate information they need, but also to recognise the tangential and linked information which might shed a completely different light on their enquiries. So when, in 1994, Warne decided to develop a database system for the Archive, it was a step towards making the collections more accessible in many different ways.

Thankfully we had a head start in this considerable task. The vast majority of the Beatrix Potter resources have been lovingly preserved, sensibly classified and documented, and the work on managing the collections had begun at a very early stage, thanks to Leslie Linder. Linder, an engineer by profession, discovered Beatrix Potter in about 1945, when he took on the responsibility for running the children's library at his local church, and his interest in her work absorbed him for most of the rest of his life, until his death in 1973. He worked tirelessly on the Beatrix Potter collections and established much of what we today regard as the heart of the resource, collecting the core of the material now held at the Victoria and Albert Museum, cataloguing part of it and then much of the National Trust collection, and in the process creating the classification system by which we still refer to Beatrix Potter's work today. He transcribed many of her letters and published three of the foundation works on her, including *A History of the Writings of Beatrix Potter* in which he chronicles step by step the history behind each of her literary works.

It is Leslie Linder's framework of classification that has provided a reference point for indexing and cataloguing the work on the Frederick Warne database. For example, the broad categories of Early Work, Natural History, Representational Works, Background for Books and Imaginary Happenings still provide headings for the catalogues of the Linder Collection at the Victoria and Albert Museum and the Frederick Warne Archive, and they informed the classification systems we started up for the database, too. In deciding on the various levels of classification, we took into account not only the internal referencing needs of the collection, but also the external needs of our various user groups. Initially the database was set up to provide a support system only for Warne, to enable easier access to the resource for use in publications, merchandise and exhibitions. But we soon realised that the system had a broader significance, and decided to create something that would eventually be of use on a wider scale, for public access and for serious scholarly research. Warne now makes this database available to visiting curators and scholars at its offices in London, and is currently working to make it available on the internet – in fact, there has been a limited release available online from spring 2003 to certain privileged, authorised users!

The system, which was developed in conjunction with software specialists, enables access through a number of different points. The classification system was designed to enable quick access across a range of purposely-selected categories, as well as to provide unique describers for each individual image. For example, the classification number for the illustrations for *The Tale of Peter Rabbit* is 7.6 and if you do a search beginning with this number you will find all twenty-eight illustrations for the little book. On each database item entry we record units of information which describe the object – object type, size, source, the original source catalogue number and also copyright information. There is also a list of 'keywords' under which the item is indexed. For instance, on item number 7.6.9, the illustration for page 22 (2002 edition) of *The Tale of Peter Rabbit*, we have keyworded every single concrete 'thing' in the picture, such as the robin, the radish and the rabbit. There are some generics such as garden tools, as well as the more specific dibber. We have recorded the actions (in this case eating) and we also noted the broader environment and contexts, so we have Mr. McGregor's garden, and the fact that it is a published illustration and that it comes from *The Tale of Peter Rabbit*.

The picture showing 'the robin, the radish and the rabbit' etc.

These keywords are designed to provide a direct way into the work if you have no fixed idea of the image you are searching for, or if you want to capture a wide band of work on a particular subject. Thus a keyword search on *The Tale of Peter Rabbit* will find everything Beatrix ever wrote or drew about the tale. As well as the original illustrations for the book, which you would find in 7.6, the results would enable you to find enough items to compose a potted history of the development of the tale, including sketches of the real Peter Rabbit, fantasy drawings which featured him, and early editions of the published book – in all, 182 images.

We organised the keywords under headings to provide some kind of context and a form of thesaurus for the work, as well as to help prompt researchers. There are about 800 individual keywords and forty headings, some of them visual. These keyword headings are the principal way of 'segmenting' the audience appeal of the database! For example, book and merchandise designers tend to have highly specific and visual needs. A typical search requirement might involve looking under the heading 'Attitude' for items indexed with the keyword 'akimbo'. For more serious research, there are also lists of locations and people. Other keyword categories are more generic – for example, under 'mammals' is the keyword 'rabbits', as well as a host of other animals which Beatrix wrote about or drew.

The variety and interconnectedness of so much of the material in the collections can be demonstrated by making a sequence of interlinked searches. The following images come from a cross-section of different collections and are not in any way biased towards the original material in the Frederick Warne Archive. I hope that this will show how the system works and how the collections can be combined to tell stories and stimulate research into Beatrix's *œuvre*.

As a starting point there are two dusty old items, coincidentally from the Frederick Warne Archive. Why should they be so intriguing? They are a pair of Beatrix Potter's own clogs, the sturdy traditional footwear that she wore while on her farms, probably with a piece of sacking draped over her shoulders to protect her from the rain, trudging through the muddy fields to check up on her herds of sheep or perhaps just to appreciate some solitude and the beauty of the local countryside. Some of the mud is still stuck to the soles, and when we lend them for exhibition we take care to ensure that they are handled properly so that we don't lose this interesting evidence!

If we wanted to find out more about the clogs, we would do a search on 'footwear', as 'clogs' is simply too specific. The system finds 108 items, but I would like to focus on some of the more obvious clog references in Beatrix Potter's life. First of all, there is a picture of Beatrix in the 1930s, enjoying herself at an agricultural show in the Lake District. Next comes the self-portrait

These three different images of clogs are among the 108 items of 'footwear' on the Frederick Warne database

from *The Tale of Pigling Bland*, published in 1913, in which Beatrix is wearing what look suspiciously like clogs. In *The Fairy Caravan*, her book of stories published in 1929 – in the United States only, at first, because she thought they were too personal – Mistress Heelis loses her clogs, but they make their own way home! Benjamin Bunny wore clogs in the eponymous tale, leaving Mr. McGregor more than a little puzzled about the curious footprints in his vegetable garden. And an unexpected connection with clogs also emerges from this system. In the late 1890s, Beatrix recorded some Roman and post-Roman objects found in excavations in the City of London, including shoe leathers.

Leaving footwear, let us move on to a more typical example of Beatrix's work, a drawing of the trunk of a large tree. This can be found in Beatrix Potter's sketchbook of 1901, which is packed full of background sketches for *The Tale of Squirrel Nutkin*. They were drawn on what Beatrix describes as a 'big island in the middle of the lake', or Owl Island, where Old Brown in *The Tale of Squirrel Nutkin* had his house. In real life this is known as St Herbert's Island, in Derwentwater, and in the database entry both the real and the fictional locations of the sketch are recorded. A keyword search on 'St Herbert's Island' reveals many different connections in the Beatrix Potter resource. Beatrix took a wonderful photograph of an old oak that then became a sketch, and which she went on to use in a picture letter. Finally, the same oak appeared in 1903 in full colour in the Warne edition of *The Tale of Squirrel Nutkin* as the home of Old Brown. And coming back to the original source of enquiry, the sketch of the tree trunk, we can then investigate one of the details in the picture, the beautiful toadstools that appear in the foreground.

Beatrix Potter's photograph of an old oak, which became Old Brown's home in *The Tale of Squirrel Nutkin*

A search on 'toadstools' reveals a fascinating mixture of scientific and fantasy work. The scientific

Beatrix Potter's 1901 picture letter to Norah Moore, and Old Brown's home in
The Tale of Squirrel Nutkin

work includes some beautiful drawings of agarics, including one of *Agaricus augustus*, drawn in Scotland within days of Beatrix writing the famous Peter Rabbit picture letter in 1893. Also to be found here is a finished book illustration in which Squirrel Nutkin sits 'upon a beech-stump playing marbles, and watching the door of old Mr. Brown', the tree trunk as a background and the toadstools in the foreground.

Moving on from the theme of toadstools, one of the drawings created for the proposed 1905 Book of Rhymes is a lovely illustration entitled 'The Rain It Raineth Every Day', which has all the rainy atmosphere of a typical day out in the Lakes. The frog sitting on his lily pad beneath his umbrella surely has to be Mr. Jeremy Fisher, or at least one of his relatives. And I must refer here to Leslie Linder's *A History of the Writings of Beatrix Potter*, which records some interesting oral history about frogs. Following Norman's death, his older brother Harold took over the responsibility for liaising with Beatrix – and they did not always see eye to eye. When Harold Warne queried the colour of Mr. Jeremy Fisher in Beatrix's illustrations (in his opinion a frog should be green, and Jeremy was too yellow), Beatrix put her frog in a jam jar and took it all the way to the Warne office in central London to show to Harold. She must have been a little affronted at having the scientific accuracy of her drawings questioned and I think that Harold probably got what he deserved! A keyword search on 'frogs' finds more than 100 drawings of them. A similar search on 'rabbits' finds in excess of 500 records, and there are more than 450 'mice' in the system.

Interestingly, although Frederick Warne took the trouble to preserve Beatrix's letters to them, they did not keep their own letters to her in a similarly systematic fashion, so understanding precisely what took place between them can often be like piecing together an incomplete jigsaw. When I read and re-read, I gain something new each time and develop a more complete idea of what she was writing about. Then comparing the letters with images and inscriptions on photographs and artwork can help to create a fuller picture of her meaning.

As an example, a letter of 26 September 1905 to Mary, Fruing Warne's wife, provides an insight into Beatrix Potter's personal relationship with the Warne family, as well as her attitude to business dealings. We can investigate further by doing some keyword research on the database. Her letter begins: 'Thank you so much for the sweet photograph of Winifred and her little sister. I should have liked it and admired it even if they had been strangers, but I have heard Norman talk so often about the children that they seem like little friends.' Search findings into 'Winifred Warne' include thirty-three pictures, drawings and letters. Winifred was the oldest of Fruing and Mary Warne's three children. This is the 'sweet photograph' that Beatrix refers to, with Winifred on the left. It was to her that Beatrix dedicated *The Tale of Two Bad Mice*.

It is easy to imagine Beatrix as a rather solitary figure, closeted in her studio in west London, writing her books in splendid isolation. But I think that one of Beatrix's secrets was that she was really not lonely and that the 'little books' and the picture letters she wrote were her way of

Winifred and Eveline Warne in 1905

communicating with children she knew personally or as pen friends. If we read more of her letter to Mary Warne, we find that she writes about returning to Wales and to the Lakes to do some sketching, which 'has got so sadly neglected this summer'. She continues with an account of a visit to Highgate Cemetery, but she never refers directly to the key event in the last three months in all their lives which led to the sad neglect of her sketching – the sudden, early death of Norman Warne, Beatrix's editor and fiancé.

Norman was the youngest of Frederick Warne's three sons, and he doted on his nephews and nieces. His main job in the Warne company was the physical production of the 'little books', though there was little strict delineation between what the brothers did. I imagine him as being a lively, creative publisher with an infectious enthusiasm, who shared Beatrix Potter's understanding of what children found interesting and who helped her to develop her ideas.

There is a beautiful watercolour painted while Beatrix was on holiday in Wales in 1905. It is dated 24 August, the day before Norman's death, and it is this date, cross-referenced to diaries and letters, that helped us to locate where the picture was drawn. At Christmas in 1905 Beatrix wrote to Millie Warne, Norman's sister: 'I am sending you a copy of the sketch I did the last evening in the barley field . . . I try to think of the golden sheaves, and harvest; he did not live long but he fulfilled a useful happy life.' We assume that the watercolour is the sketch she refers to here. Millie and Beatrix went on to be lifelong friends and their correspondence is well documented in the Frederick Warne Archive.

This brief look into the database demonstrates how the collections can provide many different journeys for the Potter researcher and, for me, they are where Beatrix becomes real. The collections also represent an important resource to attract new audiences for her work. They were central to Warne's exhibition 'Peter Rabbit's Garden', which first appeared early in 2002 at the Smithsonian Institution National Museum of Natural History in Washington, DC, and which attracted over 400,000 visitors. Using the familiarity of Peter Rabbit as a 'hook', the aim is to encourage visitors to explore the collections and to find out for themselves about Beatrix Potter as a naturalist and conservationist.

As well as the usual display of art and other features, star attractions in the exhibition are the interactive virtual walks in Beatrix Potter's Lake District. Local landscapes shown as 360-degree panoramas are superimposed with themed icons, enabling visitors to access groupings of digital 'index cards' which contain collections material linked to the particular location on view. In addition to the more obvious book material there are links to some of the lesser-known items. Visitors spend far more than a few minutes going through these walks and they look at them in real depth – in fact there is evidence that people make repeat visits just to try out the walks again and again. I feel that people are drawn into a greater understanding of Beatrix Potter when involved in exploring the collections directly. In some ways, this is just a more accessible version of small selections of material from the database, presented in the format of walks through the countryside. It has been wonderful to see members of the public, previously only aware of Beatrix as the author of *The Tale of Peter Rabbit*, begin to explore what may have been considered to be a specialist resource, and to find it fascinating. The exhibition continues to tour the world, and in 2003 a version appeared in the UK.

While the public grows increasingly aware of Beatrix Potter, serious research continues. For example, Linda Lear, biographer of the environmentalist Rachel Carson, is currently working on a book about Beatrix Potter. She is a research professor, so is meticulous in her approach to finding out about Beatrix, and will bring many fresh perspectives to bear on our understanding of her. All of them will be substantiated and backed up by references to the material evidence, which is particularly important with such a densely documented subject where the collections and references are so widely spread.

The power of Beatrix Potter, in my opinion, lies in the accessible and familiar figure of Peter Rabbit enticing people to peep round the corner into her life, and finding there all sorts of things to inspire enthusiasms and interests, with the kind of never-ending curiosity about the world that Beatrix herself possessed and that made her into such a multi-faceted character. The material she left behind, now in the collections, is enough to fuel more than a lifetime's study, and new letters and drawings will doubtless continue to surface, making it unlikely that there will ever be the final word on Beatrix Potter's life and work.

The Challenge of Reading Beatrix Potter

Reading Beatrix Potter in the UK

LYNNE MCGEACHIE

OVER ONE HUNDRED years ago when Beatrix Potter was on holiday with her parents in Scotland, she sent a picture letter to a friend, a little boy called Noel Moore. The letter began, 'My dear Noel, I don't know what to write to you, so I shall tell you a story . . .'. With these famous and immortal words in mind today, I shall tell *you* a story about the challenge of *Reading Beatrix Potter*. Are you sitting comfortably? Then I'll begin.

Once upon a time, one dark winter's night, when snow thickly covered the garden and we were snug indoors, the telephone rang. It was Carole Crosby, UK Organiser of *Reading Beatrix Potter*. At that time, I was one of her band of enthusiastic volunteer Readers helping to spread the joy of the 'little books' and their author through the land.

But perhaps I could divert for a moment from that conversation with Carole, to a brief reminder of the history of the *Reading Beatrix Potter* project. As with so many bright ideas, the kernel of the concept (forgive the Squirrel Nutkin pun) was cracked open from simple beginnings and almost by chance. In the autumn of 1997 Marian Werner, then Secretary of the Beatrix Potter Society, was asked by staff at Ham Library near Richmond in Surrey if someone from the Society would be willing to read to very young children at their forthcoming Beatrix Potter event. Marian contacted Carole Crosby, a comparatively new Member of the Society at that time, who lived locally. Carole, although a little apprehensive at the prospect of reading to a large audience of some 120 children, nevertheless agreed. The event was a great success.

Encouraged by this, the Society decided to seize the initiative. Part of the appeal of the reading at Ham Library had been the supportive display of books, posters, balloons and publicity material kindly supplied to the library by Frederick Warne. The publisher was approached again, this time by the Society, with its plan to read the 'little books' at local schools and libraries throughout the country, if sufficient volunteers could be found. Warne agreed in principle to give its support by supplying a visual aids pack to every Reader who joined. Carole Crosby agreed to be the Readings Organiser.

Now the proof of 'the roly-poly pudding' is definitely in the eating, and this particular pudding was shared out in the April 1998 issue of the Society's *Newsletter* when the proposal was put to the Membership. Seven Members volunteered immediately and thus *Reading Beatrix Potter* was born. By the spring of 1999, twenty Readers were on board, representing thirteen counties and three London Boroughs; many reading sessions had been successfully completed and many more were in the pipeline. Requests for Readings in libraries and schools could only be answered, of course, if the volunteers were available and this remains one of the challenges we face today. *Reading Beatrix Potter* depends for its very existence on the willingness of Beatrix Potter Society Members to become Readers.

By 2001 and after two years of reading, some of us were 'old hands' and this was one reason why Carole Crosby asked me, on behalf of the Committee, if I would take over as Organiser from early March that year. She, because of personal commitments, was having to retire. I was delighted to accept and as I hung up the telephone that winter's evening I pondered the challenges ahead – 'Where Next, Peter Rabbit?'

One of the wonderful things about *Reading Beatrix Potter* is that in the UK it is a national project, with both large and small groups of children, from urban and rural places up and down the country, eager to attend their local Reading. The feedback – which we obtain in the form of a questionnaire sent to each host venue after a Reading – is vital, as we seek to try and improve *Reading Beatrix*

Two 'little book' fans after a *Reading Beatrix Potter* session at their Derbyshire Primary School in 1999

Potter and, without exception, the response has been enthusiastic and positive. The individual letters of thanks and the drawings from the children themselves that often accompany the completed questionnaire are especially welcome. *Reading Beatrix Potter* is not an academic exercise for adults, welcome though their suggestions might be. The success of the project lies in the reactions of the children who attend. Their letters, written when the excitement of the event has passed, are the barometer of whether we connected with them or not. The children are our public; their letters and their drawings, earnest and sincere and often innocently humorous, are the yardstick of our success. Children do not think too much about the sensitivities of adults. If the Reading was boring or if they did not enjoy it, then they will say so.

Importantly, the Readers are also sent a copy of the completed questionnaire to encourage and, it is hoped, to inspire them to continue the good work. Volunteer Readers are the lifeblood of *Reading Beatrix Potter*, but that lifeblood has also to be life-giving, more than just reading words from a page. I believe that the challenge of *Reading Beatrix Potter* is to make the story come to life as soon as the book is opened and the page turned. The challenge lies in seeking to communicate the unique, vitalizing, inspiring influence that shines out from the 'little books'. So, as each page is turned and the whiff of hushed anticipation is detected, then a pin drop would indeed be an unwelcome intrusion.

But can it be done? Is it possible to enthral modern children who have access to such vast choices at the click of a mouse? My answer is 'yes'. In a letter to Bertha Mahony Miller written in November 1940, Beatrix Potter (now Mrs Willie Heelis) wrote:

> I do not remember a time when I did not try to invent pictures and make for myself a fairyland amongst the wild flowers, the animals, fungi, mosses, woods and streams, all the thousand objects of the countryside; that pleasant unchanging world of realism and romance, which in our northern clime is stiffened by hard weather, a tough ancestry, and the strength that comes from the hills.[1]

For me, this short quotation encompasses much of the essence of Beatrix Potter, her work and her world. It does not matter whether the child in the audience is a Johnny Town Mouse or a Timmy Willie from the country. The 'little books' contain something for everyone.

A *Reading Beatrix Potter* workshop is also a great opportunity for children to display their knowledge and forests of hands shoot up in any question-and-answer session. I use this time to introduce a few of the less well known titles and to ask 'profound' questions such as, 'Who can tell me what delicious filling Mr. Jeremy Fisher enjoyed in his sandwiches when he set off fishing?' Then there is that well-known trio beloved by so many children – suspense, action and gruesome horror. Beatrix Potter supplies them all for us as volunteer Readers to pass on. If it is suspense you are after, just take a look at *The Tale of Samuel Whiskers*: 'He squeezed through the hole in the wall, and dragged himself along a most uncomfortably tight passage where there was scarcely any light.'

As for action, there are no holds barred in *The Tale of Mr. Tod*: 'Then Mr. Tod rushed upon Tommy Brock, and Tommy Brock grappled with Mr. Tod amongst the broken crockery, and there was a terrific battle all over the kitchen. To the rabbits underneath it sounded as if the floor would give way at each crash of falling furniture.' Often it is a gruesome horror story that really appeals and where better to look than in the same book: 'The sun had set; an owl began to hoot in the wood. There were many unpleasant things lying about, that had much better have been buried; rabbit bones and skulls, and chicken's legs and other horrors. It was a shocking place, and very dark.' And thank goodness for the relief of a happy ending and laughter at last for everyone. 'Tiddly, widdly, widdly! Pouff, pouff, puff!' as Mr. Jackson so rightly says in *The Tale of Mrs. Tittlemouse*.

For older children, *Reading Beatrix Potter* is a fine opportunity to talk about Potter herself, especially when she and Bertram were young. It is a chance for our audiences to identify with them and to discover what real children, just like them, did in their summer holidays long ago. More than a century slips past, but every child in any audience today can imagine the joy of finding an old forgotten printing press in a shed, making ink for it from soot and thick, sticky colza oil, adding more soot to improve the texture, stirring it and pouring it, oh so carefully, on to the type and then savouring the triumph of producing beautiful black and smudgy labels for jam pots. Children of today know with bewildered incomprehension, just as Beatrix and Bertram did, the ungrateful attitude of adults who then confiscate the whole thing only because it is messy!

There are other real life stories to tell, too, about Beatrix Potter when she was a little girl. For example, there is her account of old Mr Woods of Dalguise. One hot summer's day he found on his walk twenty-four buff tipped caterpillars and gathered them up into his hat to show her. Unfortunately, he forgot all about them and popped his hat back on his head to shade his eyes, caterpillars and all. When the children hear that they promptly escaped, all of them right into his hair, they shriek with appalled delight. Then they discover that when she was old enough, Beatrix learned to *drive*. Not a car, though, but a pony and trap. And so the magic develops and modern children become involved and entranced.

With Potter's 'little books' and exquisite artwork before us at Readings, we discover other things together. Quite subconsciously the beauty of nature is revealed as we talk about the secret lives of her animals. With bated breath we know the wide-eyed awe of finding a bird's nest full of warm eggs and how important it is to creep away quietly in case the mother forsakes them. We read *The Tale of Jemima Puddle-Duck* and somehow we look at foxgloves in a different way ever afterwards. We know just what Peter Rabbit's cosy underground home was like and, because of a Potter painting, we look out for bats at dusk, steering past us by radar at top speed. To quote from one little group, 'Reading Beatrix Potter is cool'. They meant it and they want to know more. Furthermore, the so-called 'difficult language' does not bother the children who come to Readings. It is great fun guessing just what a conservationist might be and how we, too, can become good conservationists, just like Beatrix Potter. Difficult language is not 'soporific': it is a 'discover the meaning' game.

Information about the *Reading Beatrix Potter* project is often passed on by word of mouth. A playgroup leader who had heard good things about the Society's project of 'reading to primary school age children' contacted me one day, wondering if the programme would be suitable for pre-school age children who could not yet read. I had no hesitation in accepting the challenge and I went along to read *The Tale of Peter Rabbit* to the little group.

When everyone is clustered round chattering about Beatrix Potter, asking questions, intent upon selecting the right crayon to colour Jemima Puddle-duck's bonnet or just sitting cross-legged on the floor absorbed and listening, this is what *Reading Beatrix Potter* is all about. As the story comes to an end and I have to say that we have run out of time for the day and the response is 'Aaw', then 'The Challenge of Reading Beatrix Potter' has been met in full. Not long ago, as he was pulling on his coat to leave after a Reading, one little boy tugged my sleeve and said shyly, 'That was a lovely story'. I smiled and asked him if he had already known about Beatrix Potter and her stories. He shook his head. He had never heard of her before, he told me, but he was glad he had now. In a letter sent to Mrs W. Ferguson in October 1910 Beatrix wrote, 'I think I have little friends all over the world.'[2] *Reading Beatrix Potter* proves that she was right.

1 Taylor, Judy (ed.), *Beatrix Potter's Letters*, London: Frederick Warne, new edition, 2001, p. 423
2 Ibid., p. 186

Reading Beatrix Potter in the United States

DALE SCHAFER

> 'As I walk'd by myself,
> And talked to myself,
> Myself said unto me'[1]

IT WAS WITH a great deal of excitement that the *Reading Beatrix Potter* program was started in the United States, in response to the huge success of the scheme in the United Kingdom. In July 2001 all the 313 American Beatrix Potter Society Members were sent a letter, outlining the program and asking if they might be interested in becoming Readers. By the following year I had received seventy requests for more information and with my response I included a questionnaire asking, among other things, how many libraries and schools were within easy access, how often the volunteer would be prepared to read, what was their experience as a Reader. The thirty-five Members who responded to this and agreed to be Readers were then asked to let me know when a Reading was scheduled, approximately how many children were expected to attend, and they were provided with a letter for the librarian or teacher organizing the event to help give us feedback. Items to enhance their Readings followed – a set of the Bridget Welsh Donaldson worksheets specially prepared for the Society, together with Peter Rabbit bookmarks, a Peter Rabbit Activity Kit and a small Beatrix Potter biography, all graciously supplied by Frederick Warne/Penguin Putnam from the New York office.

By the summer of 2002 thirty-one of those volunteers had held Readings in classrooms and libraries throughout the United States and there had been a total of over one hundred Readings to thousands of children from ages four through twelve (preschool through sixth grade). Readings had been held in nineteen out of the fifty states and the audiences had ranged from three to over one hundred and fifty young children, together with many older children and adults.

Our Readers have also been actively engaged in a wide variety of other activities. As well as regular weekly Readings in local libraries or schools, some

Readers have visited the classrooms of their grandchildren or have held Readings in their own classrooms or libraries. They have gone to senior citizen homes, garden clubs, book stores, and even a librarians' association meeting. One member has set up a wonderful program for children, after successfully applying for a County Community Foundation Grant.

The challenges of coordinating *Reading Beatrix Potter* are many. Firstly, since the United States is so large, one of my challenges is to keep in touch with Readers both before and after they do a Reading. Some Readers schedule their Readings in libraries or schools without notifying me beforehand, so I have been unable to send the support material in time. Secondly, dated reports need to be returned in a timely manner from the Reader, together with the questionnaire completed by the librarian or teacher organizer. Thirdly, some Readers are without the large format books that are so helpful with the larger groups and these are increasingly difficult to find. Fourthly, some Readers feel that they should have some card to identify them as official Readers from the Society when they make the initial contact for a Reading. Fifthly, the cost of the program is a problem, basically the cost of the mailings. Sending items through the United States postal system can be very expensive. And sixthly,

Sarah Hudgens telling the children about Beatrix Potter at River Forest Public Library, Illinois, 2002

does the fact that some Readings take place in venues other than schools, libraries or book stores need to be addressed?

The challenges concerning a standard Reading seem to be minimal. Readers have had no problem in setting them up, finding schools and libraries who are excited to have the program. Many Readers are well equipped with their own Beatrix Potter materials and visual aids are numerous. Nearly everyone has their own copies of the 'little books', and many also have collections of figurines, tea sets and china, stuffed animals, books, posters, pictures of the many places Beatrix visited, lived in or painted, videos, worksheets and so on. Some librarians and teachers who host Readings do remark on the scarcity of the large format books and suggest that perhaps more programs, possibly with photographs of original Beatrix Potter sights and paintings, could be delivered in Power Point presentations or as slides on a screen. However, on the whole the suggestions for improvement are few and the positive comments are many and delightful.

I have been told that some of the Readers are 'true storytellers'. In fact, many of them are professional storytellers who memorize the 'little books', thus echoing Beatrix's words to Mrs J. Templeman Coolidge in her letter of December 9, 1929, concerning Anne Carroll Moore, 'There is nothing like the Horn Book or like Miss Moore's organization of storytellers to direct the choice of children's reading in this country.'[2]

Our Readers also make each Reading unique in their own special way. Some dress up as Beatrix Potter, others talk about her life before they begin their Reading, and afterwards children ask questions, draw, write, present plays, participate in teas, and often do crafts. It is particularly noteworthy that the Readers show such enthusiasm, have gentle manners, and are so profoundly knowledgeable about the life of this fantastic lady.

There have been many exceptional Beatrix Potter Readings in the US, but one needs special mention. It came about quite unexpectedly when Teresa Maurer of Bryan, Texas, was asked to do a Reading at The George W. Bush Presidential Library and Museum in College Station, Texas. Teresa is a member of the Storytelling Guild at the Library and she read to the one hundred and forty students from Rock Prairie Elementary School who were in attendance at the Presidential Library. She shared with them the life of Beatrix Potter, *The Tale of Peter Rabbit*, *The Tale of Benjamin Bunny* and *The Tale of Mr. Jeremy Fisher*. Then it was the turn of the former First Lady, Barbara Bush, who followed with a terrific reading of Dr Seuss's *Horton Hatches the Egg*! Teresa had the privilege of meeting Barbara Bush and telling her about the *Reading Beatrix Potter* program, both in the United Kingdom and the United States. She presented the former First Lady with one of the Society's *Newsletters* and had her picture taken with her. This is just one example of the enthusiasm that our Readers give to children and adults in sharing their love for Beatrix Potter.

But what of the future of *Reading Beatrix Potter*? The appeal of Beatrix's art and storytelling is overwhelming and will last from generation to generation. The desire to hear the 'little books' appears to be self-perpetuating. Beatrix wrote to Bertha Mahony Miller on 19 March 1942, 'I received your letter of Feb 16th yesterday and about at the same time the Jan–Feb Horn Book with your fine tribute to Anne Carroll Moore. It could not be better. What a wonderful, purposeful life of achievement – purposeful because she has had an aim all throughout her career. I have just made stories to please myself because I never grew up.'[3]

How fortunate for us that Beatrix never grew up! We would have missed out on her wonderful stories, her exquisite drawings, and her matter-of-fact, straightforward way of sharing the beauty she saw through a childish eye. In her *Journal* of 2 October 1894, Beatrix shares with us, in words of innocence:

> I am sure, driving for miles among these lonely cornfields and deep silent woods, and on the grassy slopes of the still more quiet hills, I have thought the whole countryside belonged to the fairies, and that they come out of the woods by moonlight into the fields and on to the dewy grass beside the streams. There are not many hedgehogs, which are fairy beasts, but there are the green sour ringlets whereon the ewe not bites, and how without the aid of the fairy-folk of fosterland could there be so little mildew in the corn?[4]

The goals of the Society, to promote the study and appreciation of the life and works of Beatrix Potter, are accomplished by our US Readers through the *Reading Beatrix Potter* program. The question 'Where Next, Peter Rabbit?' the title of the Tenth International Conference, has been already answered in the US by Society Readers and the children who are their audience. Beatrix's 'little books' will be in the hands, minds and hearts of generations to come, and the future of the *Reading Beatrix Potter* program here will be secure.

---

1   Potter, Beatrix, *The Fairy Caravan*, London and New York: Frederick Warne, 1929
2   Morse, J.C. (ed.), *Beatrix Potter's Americans: Selected Letters*, Boston, MA: The Horn Book, 1982, p. 31
3   Ibid., p. 17
4   Linder, Leslie (ed.), *The Journal of Beatrix Potter*, London: Frederick Warne, new edition 1989, p. 357

Developing Children's Responses to the 'Little Books' Using Worksheets

BRIDGET WELSH DONALDSON

THE CONCEPT OF using worksheets for *Reading Beatrix Potter* began with my involvement in February 1999, when my youngest daughter's primary school class were studying Beatrix Potter as part of a topic on 'Famous People'. Having read in a Society *Newsletter* about the scheme, which had just begun in libraries, I wondered whether some of the material they were using might enable me to help the children, aged between four and seven.

Marian Werner and Carole Crosby kindly arranged for me to have a Reader's pack and with it came a questionnaire asking just how many libraries I was able to read in! My first Reading was in my daughter's class at school and since then all my Readings have been in infant departments of schools. After visiting several schools I realised that it would be a great advantage in developing the children's responses to the 'little books' if there were some worksheets to follow up the Readings. So I began to design worksheets for children in the four-to-seven-year age group, and it is now clear that this is the age range for which the majority of Society Readers hold their sessions.

The National Curriculum for England and Wales requires children in primary school to share the reading of texts as a whole class together with their teacher, and this is often practised by displaying a large-format book. As *The Tale of Jemima Puddle-Duck* was the only tale I had in this format, it was the book I always chose to read first and the one for which I produced the first worksheets. *The Tale of Johnny Town-Mouse* and *The Tale of Mr. Jeremy Fisher* followed soon after, as I had obtained copies of these in the Picture Puffin editions, which are larger than the standard 'little books'. It then became a priority to produce sheets for *The Tale of Peter Rabbit* and I went on to design sheets for *The Tale of Mrs. Tiggy-Winkle*.

This is a summary of the ideas on which the twelve worksheets were based. In England and Wales children usually start school at the age of four to five, entering what is referred to as the Foundation Stage, and these are some of the curriculum requirements at this stage:

- to retell familiar stories, giving the main points in sequence
- to write labels or captions for pictures or drawings
- to use experience of stories as a basis for independent writing
- to gain phonic knowledge through reading letters that represent the sounds of 'a' to 'z', and through writing each letter in response to each sound
- to read on sight a range of familiar words, e.g. words from favourite books.

The next stage is for children aged five to seven in school Years 1 and 2. Some of the required objectives here are:

- to retell stories, giving the main points in sequence, and to pick out significant incidents
- to identify and describe characters, expressing own views and using words and phrases from texts
- to write character profiles; for example, making posters using key words and phrases that describe or are spoken by characters in the text
- to use capital letters for the personal pronoun 'I', for names and at the start of a sentence
- to make simple picture story books with sentences, modelling them on basic text conventions, such as the book cover, the author's name, the title and the layout
- to describe story settings and incidents and relate them to their own experience and that of others
- to reinforce and apply their word skills through shared and guided reading
- to use phonological, contextual, grammatical, and graphic knowledge to work out, predict and check the meaning of unfamiliar words and to make sense of their meaning.

When my sheets were ready, I was advised that I should show them to Frederick Warne, as they contained copyright material. This resulted in Warne usefully 'tweaking' the design here and there and then supplying beautifully clear and finished master copies from which it would be easy to duplicate.

There is not room here to explain each separate worksheet, so I have chosen to examine in detail four of the sheets designed for *The Tale of Peter Rabbit*, but in all cases they should only be used following the reading of the book.

The first two are for younger children. Sheet 1 covers captions and picture sequences. This reinforces the retelling of the tale and gives the opportunity of recapturing the main points in the sequence. The child reads or has each caption read to them, then draws the appropriate pictures. Sheet 2 encourages word and picture matching, helping with sight vocabulary. Older children can develop their understanding of the story and characters on Sheet 3 by designing a 'wanted' poster, and Sheet 4 is a fun session using a word search.

Name _____ Date _____

THE TALE OF PETER RABBIT
Draw some pictures to go with the story.

1. Peter Rabbit lived with his Mother and sisters in a sand-bank underneath a big fir-tree.

2. One morning he was very naughty and ran straight away to Mr McGregor's garden. First he ate some lettuces.

3. Mr McGregor ran after him waving a rake. Peter was frightened and hid in a can.

4. Peter slipped under the gate and was safe at last in the wood. When he got home his mother put him to bed.

© Frederick Warne & Co., 1901, 2001

Sheet 1

Name _____ Date _____

The Tale of Peter Rabbit
Match the pictures to the words.

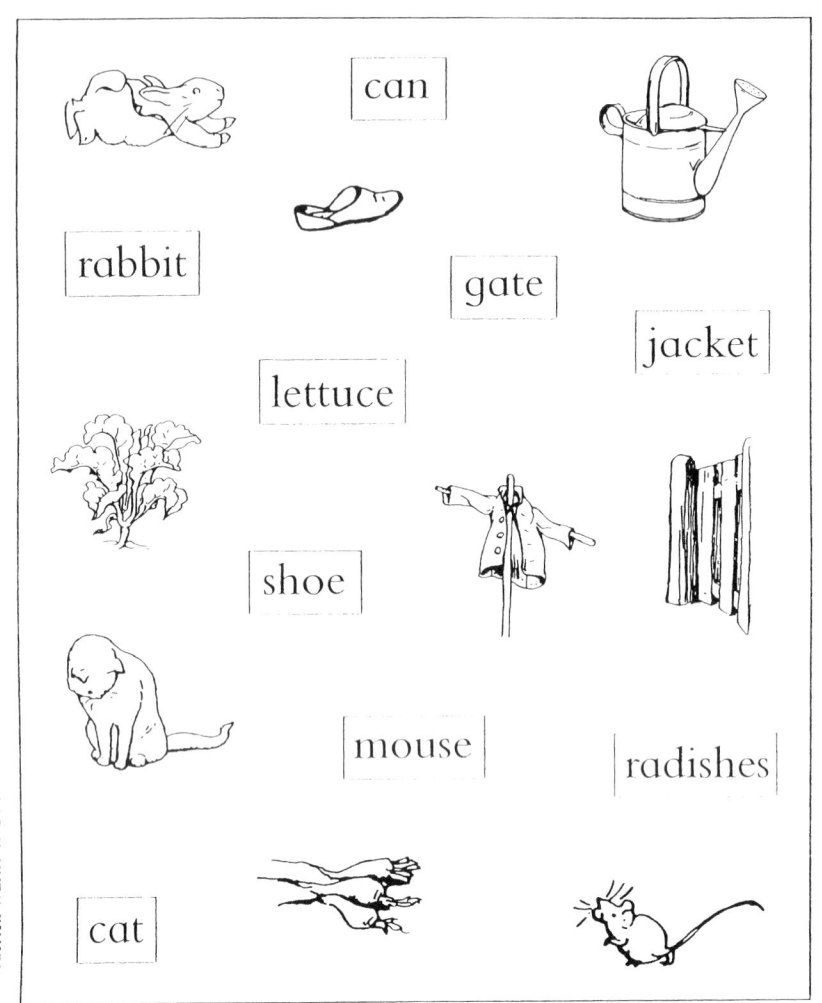

can

rabbit

gate

jacket

lettuce

shoe

mouse

radishes

cat

Sheet 2

Name .... Date ....

The Tale of Peter Rabbit
Design a 'Wanted' poster for Peter Rabbit
and suggest a reward.

WANTED!
By Mr McGregor

PETER RABBIT

For ....
....
....

Reward ....
....!

Sheet 3

Name _____ Date _____

THE TALE OF PETER RABBIT
PETER RABBIT'S WORD SEARCH

Can you help Peter find 15 words from
'The Tale of Peter Rabbit' in this word search?
Look for words going up, down, forwards, backwards
and diagonally. To help you the words are listed below.

```
n  l  s  z  t  t  x  a  r  b  f  q  x  g  n
a  r  n  h  e  i  b  u  r  e  z  h  b  k  e
d  v  s  k  o  x  v  p  w  a  h  b  l  n  d
s  c  c  b  w  e  i  p  o  n  k  t  a  u  r
r  a  b  b  i  t  s  h  o  s  m  c  o  h  a
j  q  e  s  r  e  t  s  i  s  u  j  y  m  g
e  t  a  g  d  v  a  w  v  k  n  g  r  l  n
t  c  n  p  n  u  n  l  v  k  q  d  a  z  w
p  r  i  n  l  g  e  y  f  a  h  o  d  e  c
b  e  d  u  w  t  y  e  v  y  u  o  i  i  k
l  x  o  j  t  m  u  l  k  h  c  w  s  u  v
a  p  s  u  o  g  r  f  k  a  s  x  h  d  k
h  o  c  u  g  b  r  s  h  v  r  y  e  h  i
h  e  s  a  a  p  q  u  l  f  h  q  s  x  i
s  e  p  y  h  k  y  j  c  y  u  u  z  a  n
```

beans   jacket   bed
lettuces   shoes   can
radishes   sister   garden
mouse   wood   mother
rabbit   rake   gate

Sheet 4

Beatrix Potter Overseas

Peter Rabbit in Russian

NINA DEMOUROVA

BEATRIX POTTER, alas, is very little known in Russia, though she has some staunch admirers among the English-reading public, including the present writer. It is not that she is too English for the Russian taste, for writers as English as Lewis Carroll and C.S. Lewis, or G.K. Chesterton and Evelyn Waugh, to name only a few, are well known and loved in Russia. I think the explanation, so far as these things can be explained rationally, should be sought partly in the accidents of the Russian social and political background and partly in the very special type of Beatrix Potter story, which differs greatly from the Russian animal tale.

The traditional Russian animal tale is mostly of two types: that of the folklore variety which concerns itself with peasant life; and that of the naturalistic type in which the life and habits of real animals are depicted. Of course, there are also fables, and, more or less recently, a new variety has appeared which for lack of a better word I shall describe as lyrical. In this type of animal tale the author's emotions and thoughts are projected upon the simple events of animal life. The best among these particular authors is Sergei Kozlov. Members of the older generation may have seen an animated film based on his story 'The Little Hedgehog in the Mist', with cartoons by Yuri Narstein, which has won all possible international prizes and has been shown in many countries, including England, France and Japan. It is, I am told, now also available on video.

Even from this very short description one can see that, if taken separately, each Russian variety of animal tale has certain similarities with Beatrix Potter's tales, although the general idea of the Russian animal tale is very different from that of Beatrix Potter's. But then even in England Beatrix Potter is unique!

During the Soviet days all publishing was done by the State and viewed as a very important aspect of political and ideological education. To be published at all, books had to be 'politically correct' from the Communist point of view, which was much more serious than today's political correctness, and the censor operated at all levels of publishing. Children were fed books about Lenin and Stalin and other Communist leaders and 'heroes', as well as stories in which children acted so as to prove that they were true Communists. One of the best-known of these books was the story of Pavlik Morozov who went to the KGB to inform against his own parents, with the result that they were exiled to Siberia. All of these, and similar, books were read and studied at school. Occasionally certain classics were published, as well as those rather horrible books, but mostly they were old familiars from before 1917, the time of the coup, when the Bolshevics came to power.

So it is not at all surprising that only two of Beatrix Potter's tales were published in the seventy years of the Soviet regime (1917–86), and they were *The Tale of Peter Rabbit* and *The Tale of Mrs. Tiggy-Winkle*. The former came out as a retelling under the title *Piter Krolik*, with Beatrix Potter's name not even mentioned; it was later broadcast on the radio during the children's hour. The text was changed to make it more acceptable to Russian audiences and it was a great success.

The Russian edition of *The Tale of Mrs. Tiggy-Winkle* appeared a few years later, as a 'retelling from the English by O. Obraztsova'. Beatrix Potter's name was there on the cover, but 'Beatrix' was changed to a more familiar 'Beatrice'. There were changes in the text, too, and Mrs. Tiggy-winkle became 'Ukhty-Tukhty', the first word being derived from a Russian word signifying heavy breathing or a sigh of satisfaction.

Neither of these two stories was reissued in later years, the main reason being that the book policy was tightly controlled and only very few houses were allowed to publish books for children. And that was all of Beatrix Potter that came out in Russia before 1986 – the beginning of 'perestroika'.

With the fall of the Communist regime, private publishing, freed from the dictates of the State, began to develop very quickly, and new publishers naturally turned their attention to Beatrix Potter's tales. But the difficulty lay with the pictures, for it is very expensive in Russia to print a children's book with good colour illustrations. What with the official rate of inflation at fifteen per cent per year, the price of petrol and electricity going up drastically all the time, a newly-introduced twenty-per-cent tax which is levied on all wages paid, and so on, publishers quite often feel reluctant, or they simply cannot afford, to buy the many pieces of film needed from which to print even a single

The 1989 Detskaya Literatura edition of *The Tale of Mrs. Tiggy-Winkle* (*left*) and the *Adventures of the Rabbit Called Peter,* Mir rebenka, 1998 (*right*)

Beatrix Potter book. So they try to solve the problem in their own way. When the old retelling of *The Tale of Mrs. Tiggy-Winkle* was issued by Detskaya Literatura in 1989, new illustrations were commissioned from a Russian artist I. Nakhova and in them Lucie appears as a Russian village girl of a century ago.

And so it goes on. One publisher who issued a bilingual English and Russian edition of two of the tales together had the original illustrations copied by hand and enlarged; needless to say the result was rather hideous (*The Tale of Peter Rabbit* and *The Tale of Jemima Puddle-Duck*, translated by O. Grigorieva, Moscow: Soglasie, 1994). Another publisher had illustrations, more modestly, in black and white, which was perhaps only slightly better (*Krolik Piter and Other Stories*, retold by Mikhail Grebnev, illustrated by Galina Kozhemyakina, Moscow: Semiya shkola, 1994). And a third commissioned illustrations with a Walt Disney look (*Adventures of the Rabbit Called Peter* by Beatrisa Potter, translated by M. Inge-Vechtomova, illustrated by Denis Chenov, St Petersburg: Mir rebenka, 1998).

It was in the mid-1990s that I met Alexei Zakharenkov, a young and energetic publisher from St Petersburg who expressed a desire to collaborate with me in the publishing of some English children's books. When he asked me what

I would like to do – he has beautiful manners, which is rather rare among the publishers – I immediately answered, 'A collection of Beatrix Potter's tales with the original illustrations'. One cold winter evening, on one of his regular visits to Moscow, we spent a lovely time talking about Beatrix Potter. I showed him different editions of her tales, her diaries, the books about her and her work, and he was completely fascinated, saying that he *must* find the funds to buy the films of the illustrations. He approached a number of people for financial support and he even had a pasted-up dummy prepared to show to potential distributors. Then came August 1998 and the fall of the Russian rouble. The market collapsed and the publishing house had to close down. Six of the translations I had already completed were eventually published in an All-Russia Library for Foreign Literature magazine – but that was all. However, the pasted-up dummy that the nice-mannered publisher gave me still exists!

I will not tire you with the complete saga of our attempts to have the work of Beatrix Potter published in Russia in the way she deserves and in the way she should be published. I can only say that I do hope the day will come when I shall be able to send The Beatrix Potter Society copies of her works in Russian that are as good as those published in the UK.

Although Beatrix Potter is a delight to translate, she does present a number of difficulties, even for an experienced translator. Her stories appear to be very simple on the surface; she writes in short, formal, clear-cut sentences touched with gentle (or sometimes not so gentle) irony, but hers is a simplicity which is not easy to render into a foreign tongue, especially into Russian with its many long words. And Beatrix Potter's work is, of course, very English. One of the greatest difficulties the translator faces is how to render this Englishness into Russian without turning the tales into ordinary Russian animal stories. At the same time, how does the translator avoid 'Russification' of the manner and style and yet end up with a text that is clear, understandable and enjoyable for the young reader?

The cover of Alexei Zakharenkov's pasted-up dummy for *The Tale of Mrs. Tiggy-Winkle*

I shall just mention a few of the strategies that I used while working on my translations. The first concerns the choice of the personal pronouns in the dialogue. Addressing a person in Russian, one must choose between two forms: *vy* and *ty*, which roughly correspond to 'you', both polite in singular and plural, and 'thou' which is only singular. The choice between the singular *vy* and *ty* depends on the relationship between the speakers and the social and emotional background of the situation. *Ty* is used between relatives and close friends and also between equals in social standing and age, though children in the nineteenth century (and sometimes even now) use *vy* when talking to their parents. So the *ty–vy* system must be thought out very carefully because so much depends upon it. In Russian animal tales everybody addresses each other using *ty*, but that will not do for Beatrix Potter, who was given the title of 'the Jane Austen of the nursery' upon very good grounds.

So, after very careful thinking, this is what I decided to do. In *The Tale of Tom Kitten* Mrs. Tabitha Twitchit naturally speaks to her naughty offspring using the informal *ty*, which is usual in families. Moppet, Mittens and Tom Kitten do not say anything to their mother in the story but were they to address her they would, in my opinion, use not the familiar *ty* but the more formal *vy*.

In *The Tale of Jemima Puddle-Duck* the gentleman with sandy-coloured whiskers uses a formal mode of address while talking to Jemima, 'Madam' being a clear indication of this ('"Madam, have you lost your way?"'). But later, at the very end of the tale, he would probably use a less formal *ty* when he says, '"Come into the house as soon as you have looked at your eggs. Give me the herbs for the omelette. Be sharp!" He was rather abrupt and Jemima Puddle-duck had never heard him speak like that.' On the other hand Jemima would have addressed him formally, for he is a gentleman, while she is just a puddle-duck!

Another example in the same book is in the episode with the collie-dog Kep, who is shown looking down on the simple Jemima in the illustration when he asks her, ' "What are you doing with those onions? Where do you go every afternoon by yourself, Jemima Puddle-duck?"' In Russian he would most certainly use *ty* because, firstly, he is so much superior to Jemima according to the kitchen hierarchy, and, secondly, because she is, as Beatrix Potter says, 'a simpleton'. This device of discriminating between various forms of address helps to recreate Beatrix Potter's very English atmosphere of social difference which is new to the young Russian reader.

The second translation strategy I should like to mention concerns the care that must be taken in translating the various figures of speech that Beatrix

Potter uses. One of the difficulties for Russians is English understatement, something that translators tend to skip or even to correct. Beatrix Potter, unexpectedly, does not use it as much as, say, Lewis Carroll or Kenneth Grahame, but when she does use it, it is unforgettable! Look at *The Tale of Peter Rabbit*, for example, when old Mrs. Rabbit warns her children not to go into Mr. McGregor's garden: '"Your Father had an accident there; he was put in a pie by Mrs. McGregor."' In the few existing Russian translations I discovered that more than once 'the accident' had been translated as 'great misfortune', which does not do justice to Beatrix Potter's wonderful humour. I need hardly say that in my translation I tried to keep as close to the original as possible.

The third strategy is the care of choosing just the right words. Beatrix Potter, as a rule, employs very simple language. Her particular impression of formality is mostly created by the occasional usage of slightly archaic or highly literary words. In *The Tale of Tom Kitten* Mrs. Tabitha Twitchit speaks very simply to her children, whether it be on topics of everyday life or while giving them directions: '"Now keep your frocks clean, children! You must walk on your hind legs. Keep away from the dirty ash-pit, and from Sally Henny-penny, and from the pig-stye and the Puddle-ducks."' But when she sees them with no clothes on she says, '"My friends will arrive in a minute, and you are not fit to be seen; I am affronted."' This 'affronted' presents a certain difficulty for the translator, as it contrasts so much with the rest of the vocabulary, being archaic and highly literary. Moreover it is a word that only an educated person would use! So the translator must look for a word with similar connotations in Russian, not pass it over or just 'render the meaning'. There are numerous other examples but let me just quote one more, which comes a little later in the same tale: 'Somehow there were very extraordinary noises over-head, which disturbed the dignity and repose of the tea-party.'

There are many other things concerning the translating of Beatrix Potter that I should love to discuss in detail, but they will have to wait until another time. For instance, how does one tackle those allusions to characters that are familiar to English readers but not to Russian ones, as in *The Tale of Mrs. Tiggy-Winkle* where Beatrix Potter mentions both Miss Muffet and Jenny Wren? Fortunately, however, there are some allusions in the stories which our children know very well, such as Mother Ladybird in *The Tale of Mrs. Tittlemouse* and the crooked penny in *The Tale of Two Bad Mice*. And what degree of freedom is permissible in rendering alliteration, as in *The Tale of Timmy Tiptoes* where the two friends are heard to sing, '"For the diddlum day,/Day diddle dum di!/Day diddle diddle dum day!"'? Or question of questions, how to approach the names? Should they be translated into Russian, or just transliterated? It seems to me that in the case of Peter Rabbit or Tom Kitten the answer is clear, but what about Mrs. Tiggy-Winkle and Timmy Tiptoes?

But I must stop here. I can only say that I consider myself extremely fortunate that among the many books I have translated into Russian there are such delightful masterpieces as *The Tale of Mrs. Tiggy-Winkle*, *The Tale of Squirrel Nutkin* and *The Tale of Tom Kitten*.

A Case of Distortions

SHIN-ICHI YOSHIDA

I AM HAPPY TO say that in Japan we now have the complete series of Beatrix Potter's 'little books', together with *The Fairy Caravan* and the selection of her miniature letters, *Affectionately Yours, Peter Rabbit*. These authorised editions have come out at intervals since 1971, but before then several 'translations' of the Peter Rabbit books were available – though they were published with illustrations that were not by Beatrix Potter.

The earliest translation, as far as I know, was *The Tale of Tom Kitten*, which was published in February 1926 in a magazine for children called 'Kodomonotomo' or 'Children's Friend'. It was really an adaptation rather than a translation and the illustrations were traced from the originals by Kiichi Okamoto, a popular illustrator of the time. Both story and pictures were set out on one double-page spread in eleven scenes, with the illustrator's name printed in very small type at the bottom of the page. As the name of Beatrix Potter was nowhere to be seen, it appeared as if the story had been written by the illustrator – a regrettable situation, but then it was over seventy-six years ago. The Japanese title of the story was *The Naughty Kittens and the Ducks Who Lost Their Clothes*.

Beatrix Potter was very particular about clothes, not only in *The Tale of Tom Kitten* but in all her books, as Peter Hollindale has pointed out in 'Animal Stories since Beatrix Potter and her Influence on the Genre' (from *Beatrix Potter as Writer and Illustrator*, Beatrix Potter Studies VIII). In *The Tale of Tom Kitten* she particularly focuses on clothes, mocking Mrs. Tabitha Twitchit as she tries to show how well-behaved and charming her kittens are by dressing them neatly. But Tabitha Twitchit ignores the true character of children and so is disgraced

1 Three little kittens were happy together in the sun.
2 Their mother cat arrived and said, 'Now you must come home, as we have guests. I will dress you neatly.'
3 'Oh, dear, your face is dirty, Bobie.' His mother scrubbed his face with a sponge.
4 There was great trouble with the kittens' clothes. 'Oh, what shall I do?'
5 'It has all worked out very nicely and you are now looking lovely.' Bobie was in blue, Happy in pink and Timmy in white.
6 But the three kittens were very naughty and they immediately took off their clothes, finding them a nuisance.
7 The three kittens stood in a row on the garden wall and under the wall came three puddle-ducks.
8 So the kittens gave their clothes to the ducks.
9 Quack, Guack and Goosie set off home, wearing the clothes and keeping step.
10 When the three ducks reached their pond, they dived under the water, but soon they rose to the surface in confusion.
11 Their clothes had disappeared. Although they searched and searched for them, it was in vain. They have been looking for them ever since.

The Japanese edition of *The Tale of Tom Kitten* appeared as *The Naughty Kittens and the Ducks Who Lost Their Clothes*. The story reads from top right (1), down each column, ending with bottom left (11) and ridiculed before her guests, especially when Tom Kitten is pictured wearing a blue bonnet. It is as if he is saying, 'You insisted on my wearing my best clothes, but I think I look much better in this.' It is a bitter sarcasm, a severe irony. Then at the very end of the book, as a kind of sequence to this event, the silly Puddle-ducks are made to look a laughing-stock by losing the kittens' clothes, which they had put on. Of course, this scene is also Beatrix Potter's explanation of why ducks stand on their heads, rather like Kipling's story of how the elephant got his trunk, but it is, as well, her final word about clothes.

The 1926 Japanese version of the story not only loses the theme of the original but misses the irony and humour completely. *The Naughty Kittens and the Ducks Who Lost Their Clothes* is just a story of three kittens who gave their clothes to the ducks and of the ducks who lost them. It is a supreme example of the *perils* of translating Beatrix Potter.

The next example of distortion in translation relates to *The Tailor of Gloucester*, published in 1966, translated by Isoko Hatano and illustrated by Hiroshi Inoh. The picture on page 49 (of the Warne edition) is one of my favourite Beatrix Potter illustrations. The cat Simpkin, alerted to his unkindness to the tailor by the mice and by the sound of Christmas in the air, has retrieved the silk from the teapot and put it on the tailor's bed. In the text Beatrix Potter writes, 'When the tailor awoke in the morning, the first thing which he saw, upon the patchwork quilt, was a skein of cherry-coloured twisted silk, and beside his bed stood the repentant Simpkin!' And the picture shows the 'repentant' Simpkin beside the tailor's bed, holding his cup of morning tea [see over]. It is a remarkable illustration of a word that might well be a difficult one for young children to understand.

Our translator, however, paraphrased this part of the story into, 'The tailor awoke in the morning. The first thing he saw was a skein of twisted silk. The twist was upon the patchy and darned counterpane. Beside the tailor's bed stood the depressed Simpkin. He looked as if he was saying, "I am dreadfully sorry".' The translator was trying to explain the situation as clearly as possible without using either 'repentant' or 'repentance'. The translator also made the mistake of turning 'patchwork quilt' into 'patchy and darned counterpane', thus indicating that the tailor was poor. The illustrator has followed her lead and shown a worn-out counterpane, with a depressed cat sitting beside the bed. This kind of distortion through translation spoils the interdependent and co-operative harmony between text and illustration that is one of the most distinctive features of Beatrix Potter's 'little books'.

In contrast, Momoko Ishii made an entirely faithful translation, understanding entirely, for example, that the illustration provides the explanation for

Hiroshi Inoh's interpretation of the Tailor of Gloucester and Simpkin in the Japanese edition, and Beatrix Potter's original illustration

the word 'repentant'. While her translation of *The Tale of Peter Rabbit* was in progress in 1971, I happened to be in England and had the lucky opportunity to meet Leslie Linder. He knew that the Japanese translation was in progress and he was anxious to know whether the Japanese text would turn out to be longer. When I told him that in Japanese it usually does become longer, he said, 'That is too bad, for it is important that the text matches each page of the original.' Ninety-five-year-old Miss Momoko, when recently interviewed by a magazine, recalled the time when she was translating the book and how she took great pains to keep the Japanese text to the same number of lines as each original page so that it matched up with the opposite illustration. Leslie Linder need not have worried.

In her translation of *The Tale of Ginger and Pickles* Momoko Ishii chose to use Japanese expressions that she felt were more appropriate and more easily understood by young Japanese readers. For instance, the words 'seed wigs', 'sponge-cake', 'butter-buns' and candles called 'self-fitting sixes' are extremely English, so she substituted 'buns', 'kasutera' (a popular Japanese sponge cake), 'bread rolls' and 'handy-sized small candles'. She is indeed a flexible translator. She worked hard at translating the 'little books' into Japanese and what is also apparent to us as bystanders is that she appeared to enjoy thinking out ways of putting Beatrix Potter's highly individual style of English into Japanese. I am happy to report that Momoko Ishii's efforts are a very good example of the *pleasures* of translating Beatrix Potter.

The Perils Peter Rabbit Has Faced in Lithuania

KESTUTIS URBA

THE FIRST PERIL with which I shall start is that Peter Rabbit (Petriukas in Lithuanian) could not find his way to Lithuanian children. After all, between 1918 and 1940, Peter Rabbit was still very young and he probably did not care about the existence of an even younger independent state of Lithuania on the world map. It is the Lithuanian literary scientists, translators and teachers of that time who are to blame for the failure to discover the world created by Beatrix Potter, for in the period in question the children's literature and book publishing systems in Lithuania were still in their initial stages of formation. Although many translations of works of children's literature were published, mostly they were from the German language and so far I have not found the name of either Beatrix Potter or her books among abundant Lithuanian periodicals or literary science of that epoch.

After 1940 Lithuania nearly vanished from the map of the world altogether when it found itself behind the so-called Iron Curtain. Thus Peter Rabbit, given that he had even heard about Lithuania, would have had to go via Moscow to reach it. And maybe, maybe – as one of my acquaintances from Germany joked – he would have had to have acquired red ears even to get permission to travel to Lithuania.

Seriously, I have to say that during the fifty years of Lithuania's incorporation into the Soviet Union (1940–90), after the country was deprived of independence, the translations of literature from Western Europe and other foreign countries into Lithuanian were most often made from the Russian language. It is true that eventually there were more translations from the original languages, but in most cases a book had to come out first in Russian to be 'verified'. The work of Beatrix Potter is a typical example of such practice. In 1959 *The Tale of Mrs. Tiggy-Winkle* was published in Lithuanian as a translation from Russian but it contained pictures by the Russian painter, G. Kalaushin, rather than those by Beatrix Potter. In 1995, one small publishing house in Lithuania repeatedly reissued the same tale, but that edition was illustrated with pictures by the Lithuanian painter, Laima Skerstonaite. Her pictures are interesting but to my

The cover of the 1959 Lithuanian edition of *The Tale of Mrs. Tiggy-winkle* (*left*) and the 1995 edition of the same little book (*right*)

mind they are distant in style from those of Beatrix Potter. I am not competent to assess the translation of the text but, in my opinion, it sounds quite good and does not distort the original. It looks as though O. Obraztsova did her job of the translation into Russian fairly well, but Lithuanian children, including myself, did not have the chance to feel the true, authentic Beatrix Potter, for they could read neither her other texts nor see a single picture by her.

In 1990 Lithuania regained its independence and the road from England to Lithuania was remarkably strengthened, thus giving the green light to Peter Rabbit. It was while I was lecturing on children's literature at Vilnius University that I became aware of the importance of Beatrix Potter and of her role in the history of children's literature. At home I had a copy of *A Treasury of Peter Rabbit and Other Stories* (New York: Avenel Books, 1978) and, although the illustrations in that book were of relatively poor quality, I managed to interest both the editor of Vyturys, the main children's literature publishing house, as well as the administration of the Open Society Fund Lithuania (backed by the Soros Foundation), in them. They were launching the project 'Step-by-Step' at the time, and I persuaded them to include in it at least one book by Beatrix Potter. 'Step-by-Step' aimed to publish books for small children and the Soros Foundation funding enabled many Potter books to be bought for kindergartens.

After lengthy efforts, we at last contacted Frederick Warne (initially, we knew nothing about the copyright of Beatrix Potter) and asked their permission to publish *The Tale of Peter Rabbit*. As far as I understand the situation, it was Frederick Warne who suggested the simultaneous publication of three more titles and so, in 1998, four books by Beatrix Potter came out in the Lithuanian language, *The Tale of Peter Rabbit*, *The Tale of Two Bad Mice*, *The Tale of Mr. Jeremy Fisher* and *The Tale of Mrs. Tittlemouse*.

Now I come to the second and key peril for Peter in Lithuania, namely the peril of wrong translation. The translation of these four books was undertaken by a young translator, Viltaras Alksnėnas, who had little experience in the field and who had learned English as his third language. However, he had lived in the countryside, he has a good command of his mother tongue – both literary and colloquial Lithuanian – and, what is very important, he was very fond of the Beatrix Potter books. [He is also known as Kestutis Urba!]

Some of the difficulties in translating Beatrix Potter are the traditional ones. For instance, I believe that it is impossible to retain such word play as, 'This is a tale about a tail' (*The Tale of Squirrel Nutkin*), since in translation the homophones disappear, and I can imagine that translating the rhymed riddles and songs, which are so significant in some books by Potter, would be a real challenge. Of course, some differences also exist in the nature, geography and the details of England and Lithuania. Another essential difference undoubtedly lies in a gap of the hundred years between the world described by Potter and that of today's child. Also, the books are set mainly in the country, and with most readers today living in cities, they are not aware of many of the details that appear in her books.

The translator into Lithuanian also has a problem concerning the character of Peter Rabbit. A Lithuanian child understands the word 'rabbit' as a domestic animal; in forests and fields here they find only hares. Nonetheless, the word 'rabbit' in translation was retained, rather than 'hare', which proved to be the correct choice. Any fear that this would prevent readers from understanding the book were not justified, due to the fact that these days small children in cities hardly know either a rabbit or a hare. Some of the vegetables in the story also appear in a different context in Lithuania, but in their case one of Beatrix Potter's precise pictures accompanying the text is usually of great help. There are a number of other details that may seem strange in Lithuania, too. For instance, I do not know how one would translate the word 'patty-pan' in the book that features that object!

A translator faces particular problems when translating for the youngest child. After some years of experience, I know that translating a book for that age group is more difficult than, let us say, for teenagers. A translator must be more attentive to every detail and every word, and should be aware of how frequently a word is used in contemporary language. One mother, whose five-year-old son became a fan of Peter Rabbit, produced precise statistics for me showing how many words her son failed to understand as he listened to her reading the translation of *The Tale of Peter Rabbit*. Firstly, there were a few figurative synonyms which the translator had chosen, instead of the proper words. An example being the use of 'to peg away' or 'to be on the trot' instead of the simple 'to work'. Secondly, there were a couple of rather complicated grammatical forms, such as the use of the Past Perfect, which could have been omitted. And thirdly, there were a few items that were strange to a city child ('tool-shed' and 'sieve'). However, the mother also said that it is very good that with every book a child should find out and learn new words, but that the number of such words should not be excessive.

The translation of the character's names in the Beatrix Potter books is a very difficult job and a most serious challenge. On the other hand it can also be a pleasure, giving the translator some room for creation. Translating children's literature into Lithuanian in the first half of the twentieth century showed a tendency to change foreign names into Lithuanian ones. The present-day translation theory favours the retaining of authentic names so that the reader can 'feel' the context of the other country conveyed through them. In most cases the translator of Beatrix Potter's books cannot keep her original (authentic) names, for they would sound strange and possibly even unpleasant to a small child. However, we know that many of the names relate directly to common nouns, so it was possible to leave unchanged such a name as 'Tittlemouse', though I have no idea of what should be done with 'Mrs. Tabitha Twitchit'. To my mind both the original names and the literal translation of 'Ginger' and 'Pickles' would sound odd and silly; and the modification of such names as 'Mr. Alderman Ptolemy Tortoise' and 'Sir Isaac Newton' in *The Tale of Mr. Jeremy Fisher* was inevitable. But the name of the main character in that book remained and, from a present-day perspective, I think perhaps it was a mistake. Affricates such as 'j' are not very common in the Lithuanian language and Jeremy (Dzeremis) sounds strange to our children, some of whom would also find it difficult to pronounce. Maybe that is one of the reasons why this book is the least popular in Lithuania, at least in terms of the sales of all the four translated here?

However, the choice of Peter Rabbit's name seems to have been very successful. In Lithuanian Petriukas is similar to Peter. It is also a name that is common among Lithuanian boys, so the title of the book immediately makes

Lithuanian readers smile. I suppose that was the effect that Potter sought with the majority of her characters' names. Recently, books by Lithuanian authors have revealed a tendency to name various characters (usually in nonsense-type tales) after real children, which has aroused a certain amount of criticism from some teachers. They claim that such a practice creates a pretext to tease and hurt those children whose names occur in literature, especially if it is the negative characters who have their names. I agree that writers and translators should be careful and be aware of the right balance but I also feel that such a dramatic response, which has been the case with much of the feedback from children's literature, arises from super-pedagogical adults rather than from the children themselves.

Now I must disclose a secret about the peril that relates to the names of the Potter characters that Lithuania failed to avert. No doubt the mistake occurred owing to the difference between the two languages. Lithuanian compared to English is not so different, for instance, as Japanese, and it pertains to the same Indo-European family of languages, although it belongs to a different and rather specific branch of Baltic languages. Lithuanian is a synthetic language in which grammatical relations are more often expressed through various forms of the words, rather than through auxiliary words or a sequence of words. The grammatical category of gender is very important in the Lithuanian language. In our case it is important that the absolute majority of animal names in Lithuanian are either of feminine or masculine gender. For example, the translation of Squirrel Nutkin would present a difficulty, since in Lithuanian 'squirrel' is only feminine. The noun 'rabbit' is a similar case, as in Lithuanian it is always masculine. Therefore, the translator of *The Tale of Peter Rabbit* translated Flopsy, Mopsy and Cotton-tail as masculine names, so in Lithuania Peter Rabbit now has three brothers instead of three sisters. Only a year after the book came out one six-year-old girl pointed her finger at a picture, saying, 'Look, one jacket is blue, and the other three are red! Maybe they are girls?' It came as a thunderbolt for the young translator, too.

A year ago, I received a wonderful present from the Japanese translator, Ruriko Otsuki. It was a copy of *The Complete Tales of Beatrix Potter* (Frederick Warne & Co.) so I now know that in the next book Flopsy marries Benjamin Bunny. I also now know that many of the Potter characters travel from one book to another. It was a good lesson, that a translator must be well acquainted with the whole context of an author's works but, unfortunately, five years ago other books by Potter were not available in Lithuania. Happily, Flopsy, Mopsy and Cotton-tail are not key characters in the book and their gender is not so crucial as to prevent the reader understanding the story. Neither has the translator's mistake triggered any cultural scandal in Lithuania. (I even joked with a few friends that such a context echoes today's feminist ideas, in that one cannot emphasise the difference between boys and girls or describe girls as obedient or boring, for this contravenes the spirit of the epoch.) However, we fear what will happen when the Lithuanian translation of *The Tale of the Flopsy Bunnies* appears! And that mistake teaches one more lesson – in translating a picture book one must be very attentive, since every colour or small stroke in a picture may be significant.

Finally, I move to the third peril that Peter Rabbit may face, all because of the unimaginative approach of adults to children's literature. In preparation for this Conference I circulated a questionnaire among teachers in kindergartens. I asked what they themselves knew about Beatrix Potter either when children, or now; what the parents of the children in their care knew about this author; which books by her were the favourites of those children; what did they have to say about them; and how did the teachers as adults view these books. All the teachers wrote that neither they nor the parents had heard of this author before. They said that they mostly preferred *The Tale of Mrs. Tittlemouse* because 'it contains many didactic details about neatness and order'. All the books 'teach goodness, politeness, understanding, sensitiveness' and 'children learn how they should not behave'. According to the questionnaire, the children are least interested in *The Tale of Two Bad Mice* 'perhaps because children want to be better and do not like bad mice'. There were a few responses indicating that children of pre-school age prefer the telling to the reading of the stories, but then Beatrix Potter's tales are impossible to tell, since they contain so many details which are hard to remember even for an adult. But comments were also made that abundant details enrich children's language. What is important is that the teachers noted frequent requests for them to read the books again. They also said that the children often leafed through the books, telling their own stories from the pictures.

I was a little astonished by the feedback from the teachers about the works of Potter merely from a didactic and pedagogical perspective, using children's books to teach or moralise, for they seem to have little intuitive understanding of the artistic nature of the picture book genre. The picture book does not have a long tradition in Lithuania and is a new type of book to many adults. This may explain the didactic approach to children's literature, which I suppose has remained, not only in Lithuania. But in some responses we can see that the children on their own discover and have a quite adequate understanding of the works by Potter and I have received plenty of impressive responses, especially from families of my acquaintances, both parents and children. Four-year-old Danielius, whenever visiting his aunt, who gave him the Potter books as a present, kept saying for almost two years, 'I am Peter Rabbit!', identifying himself very sincerely with the naughty character of the book. Another acquaintance, Joris (he is eight now), sometimes played tricks on his guests. Although he was then not yet at school, he used to say to them, 'Now I will read to you', and he would bring out *The Tale of Peter Rabbit* and 'read' every page without a single mistake – having learned the text by heart when his grandfather used to read it to him. And during a walk with his parents near the Nemunas River (the largest in Lithuania), Joris, who lives in the country's second largest city, Kaunas, would argue earnestly that over there, under a pine, lived Peter Rabbit. Asked by his parents to find him, he would say that today Peter had gone to the other bank of the river.

The first authorised edition in Lithuanian of *The Tale of Peter Rabbit*, 1998, translated by Viltaras Alksnėnas

When I told my adult daughter about my trip to the Centenary of Peter Rabbit, she jokingly asked whether he was still alive. 'Yes,' I said. 'Peter Rabbit is alive. He lives both near the Nemunas and in the whole of Lithuania. It is true that in Lithuania he has got three brothers instead of three sisters, but this is a story and it is not alien to the most surprising of magic transformations.' The children of Lithuania have already become fond of Peter Rabbit, Mrs. Tittlemouse, Jeremy Fisher and the Two Bad Mice, and I am assured that they will become the dearest of childhood books to many of them, which is the biggest of pleasures to the translator of Beatrix Potter's books. I hope that all of you will wish that Lithuanian publishers and buyers become richer very soon, so that the children of Lithuania will one day be able to read other books by Beatrix Potter and thus be more often in touch with a true verbal and visual art.

Beatrix Potter's Side Shows

NICHOLAS DURBRIDGE
Chairman and CEO

IN 1984 THE Copyrights Group was appointed by Frederick Warne to handle the licensing of all the products and merchandise of Peter Rabbit and other Beatrix Potter characters around the world. Our organisation is based in the United Kingdom, but we also have offices overseas, in Hamburg, Tokyo and Melbourne, with an associated office in the United States. The role of Copyrights in licensing the characters which Beatrix Potter created is to grant licences only to those manufacturers whom we think will produce suitably high quality products. We negotiate the terms of the licence, manage the stringent approval process and finally offer advice on the marketing of the licensee's goods.

The licensing industry is a very large, lively and sophisticated business nowadays. In terms of the size of the industry overall, one-hundred-and-nine-billion-pounds-worth of licensed merchandise was sold around the world in the year 2000. Virtually anything can be licensed, not just characters from books, but famous brand names or even the local baseball or football team.

In 1984, when we started to be involved with licensing Peter Rabbit, the life cycle of a product was expected to be about three years. In the first year sales would start to rise, in the second they would peak, and then in the third there would be a downturn. At that point we would persuade the licensee to invest in new designs so that in the fourth year sales would come back up again. Nowadays, the life cycle is usually one year, and a product may be on the market for only six months. Retailers are constantly on the lookout for new products, even if the products they are currently selling are successful. As a result, Copyrights receives and turns round a considerable number of products for approval throughout the year.

As with so many things, Beatrix Potter was way ahead of her time: she was one of the first people to start character licensing – in 1903, nearly two decades before Walt Disney. This may come as a surprise, as most people in the United Kingdom tend to think of licensing, in a modern sense, as having taken off with a group of characters who appeared on television in the mid-1970s called the Wombles.

Judy Taylor's *That Naughty Rabbit: Beatrix Potter and Peter Rabbit* contains a most interesting chapter about the early years of Beatrix Potter's licensing exploits. Beatrix started with a soft toy, which she designed and made herself, and she registered the design at the UK Patent Office in December 1903. From the outset she seemed to have no qualms or hesitations about starting her 'side shows', as she called them. She thought that it was a perfectly legitimate and reasonable thing for an author or creator to extend his or her characters into other media that would give children pleasure. chap 2

Inevitably many of those media are more transitory than a book. A book will stay on a bookshelf and may be treasured for life, but a tee-shirt is worn for a year until the child grows out of it, and then it is discarded or handed down to the next child. So character merchandise by its very nature tends not to last so long. Also the merchandise usually has only one or two images featured on it, and therefore it cannot have the impact that a book does. Books contain the complete story, the drama and the humour, while merchandise is much more about design; it is about visual impact. Beatrix realised this very early on when she created her soft toy, and by the autumn of 1904 she was designing wallpaper and working on some initial designs for the Peter Rabbit Race Game, although that did not appear until much later. She contrived a painting book in 1911. In 1917 a plethora of products appeared. Beatrix was involved with the licensing of slippers in a Peter Rabbit log box, as well as handkerchiefs and bibs. A little later a tea-set was manufactured by Grimwade. There was also a series of tiles: these are very rare, but they can occasionally be found in antique shops – I found one in a shop in Australia. This all took place long before the modern age of licensing which came about with films and television.

Beatrix Potter had a long and close relationship with the publishing firm of Frederick Warne. After her death, the company took over the responsibility for licensing her works, but in the 1960s and 70s they were very cautious about what they should license and did not go out actively to seek companies to create merchandise. As a result the merchandising programme became quite small. good intro for chap 4.

When Copyrights became involved with the licensing of the Beatrix Potter characters in 1984, there were very few licensees around the world: eleven in the UK, thirteen in the USA, and just one in Japan. There were none in

87

An early piece of merchandising was the 1911 *Peter Rabbit's Painting Book*

Australia and New Zealand, although these English-speaking countries were very familiar with Beatrix Potter's 'little books'. There were none in Continental Europe, even though the books had been published in French and various other languages for many years, and there were none in South-East Asia. The North American programme was actually bigger than the British one, largely because of the influence of a man called Dick Billington, who ran the Frederick Warne office in the United States. Dick was a member of the Warne family and because he was in New York, far away from Bedford Square, he was granted a certain amount of autonomy. Early on he was approached by Eden Toys, whose President, Richard Miller, was very well connected with the baby and infant industries in the United States during the 1970s. As well as taking a licence to make soft toys, Miller also introduced a number of other companies to Frederick Warne, including some who made clothing and bedding. These companies formed the nucleus of the American licensing programme, which grew steadily and became larger and more co-ordinated than the one in the UK.

At this time the British licensees included Antioch, who made bookplates, and Cuckoobird, who produced kitchen accessories and aprons. Dragons made very up-market hand-painted furniture and still has a Beatrix Potter licence. Crabtree and Evelyn, the toiletries company, is also still in the programme today. Contrary to popular belief, the latter is not an English company, but an American one founded by a man called Cy Harvey. He did not really like licensing and was not keen to take licences, but he had two passions in life: one was corgi dogs, so he took a licence for Tasha Tudor products, as she is well-known for including corgis in her illustrations; his other passion was Beatrix Potter and Peter Rabbit, so he took a licence for Peter Rabbit.

By 1984, Eden Toys had acquired rights outside the United States and was selling in the British market. Other UK licensees included: Huntly Bourne and Stevens, a well-known English tinware company; Hunkydory, an established stationery and tin and accessory company; Metal Box, who was also making tin trays and other tin items; Royal Doulton, who manufactured the famous ceramic figurines; Supercast, who made plaster-moulding kits; and finally, Wedgwood, who created the charming children's dinner sets. Sadly, most of these companies have now gone out of business, due to economic conditions in Britain and the United States. There are very few licensees today who were in the programme eighteen years ago. The big multiple retailers now require fewer suppliers, and this has brought about global consolidation in industry.

Early on, Frederick Warne produced a Jemima Puddle-duck wooden jigsaw puzzle and, at one point, they actually had a man in the basement of Bedford Square cutting these by hand – with a jigsaw. In the 1970s Puck Toys also produced jigsaw puzzles but went out of business in the early 80s rather spectacularly, when their warehouse burnt down and the insurance company refused to pay up.

When Copyrights became involved with the licensing of Peter Rabbit, it immediately decided to bring into the programme companies whose products were relevant to babies and very young children. We started by licensing a pre-eminent company called Simplantex, manufacturers of nursery fabrics and bedding. This was followed by Vymura, who took a license for wallpaper. Children's clothing manufacturers were then approached. In those days the colours of clothing for children up to about the age of seven were Jemima pink for girls and Peter Rabbit blue for boys! Today's children's clothing is much more fashion-orientated, and there is far more variety in the colour.

Other companies who came into the programme in the mid-80s were Marks & Spencer, who took out a licence in stationery, which was, and still is, made for them by a company called Tigerprint. Golden Bear took a licence to produce a hot water bottle cover for Boots, another famous British retailer. Cloverleaf created prints for babies' and children's bedrooms. And Sari Fabrics, whose expertise was in fine printing on fabric and who produced quality goods in the kitchen accessories area, decided to have a theme based on the Ginger & Pickles shop, and developed a tea-cosy, a bag and an apron, as well as a number of other items. Table-mats were manufactured by

Taunton Vale and the origins of this enterprise are surprising, in that the company were at one time associated with the aero-engine industry, making cork gaskets. When they decided to laminate the cork circles cut out of the gaskets, they created the first laminated cork table-mats!

During this period, packaging started to play an increasingly important part in the marketing of products, and using the character of Peter Rabbit certainly enhanced sales. Copyrights was keen to market the Warne Peter Rabbit Race Game, but the licensee, HP Games, was convinced that Beatrix Potter's original game was far too complicated for children. We disagreed with them, but in the end they insisted that they wanted to do a simplified game; popular for only a few years, it is no longer available. In 1993 a superb facsimile of Beatrix Potter's own game came on to the market in a limited edition, manufactured by a British company called Traditional Games. It is expensive, but you get what you pay for. The little counters are red and green moulded cabbages, the die shaker is a genuine ceramic flowerpot, the playing pieces (also facsimiles of the originals, but not in lead) come in a little hessian bag, and the board is beautifully printed and of superb quality. This game is still available and it is very popular – proving that our judgment at the time of our initial suggestion was correct.

Across the Atlantic in 1984 Warne had licensed Dallas Alice to make tee-shirts. Fallani and Cohn made place-mats and other kitchen accessories. Green Apple produced needlework books, patterns, and pattern books for sewing. JHB International manufactured buttons. Quiltex made bedding, and a clothing company called Nanette brought out lovely dresses. Paper Art manufactured paper cups and plates, but no longer exist as a company, only as a brand name. Schmidt made wonderful and highly collectable ceramic musical boxes, but sadly they and Thomas Textile, who made playwear and baby suits, have both now gone out of business. Schumacher manufactured wall coverings and Trimfit produced clothing.

Eden Toys was dominant in the US soft toy market in the 1980s. It distributed its toys in a different way from everybody else, targeting nursery shops and department stores rather than toy shops. It did very well, and was successful until about 1996-7, when it started being heavily involved in character licensing, becoming the licensee for Teletubbies and Madeline and then taking licences for 'hot' characters. The trouble with this is that companies can sometimes get stuck with unsaleable stock when a craze fades, and as a result Eden toys went spectacularly bankrupt in 2000.

In Japan, prior to 1984, a company called Familiar had taken out a licence through Fukuikan Shoten, the publishers of the Peter Rabbit books there.

Familiar was the only Japanese Peter Rabbit licensee for many years, producing a wide range of clothing, bags and stationery which it sold through its own shops as well as through concessions in department stores, and it was very successful in the late 1970s, the 80s and the early 90s. Japanese products have always been extremely interesting and of very high quality, as the Japanese consumer is very particular about what he or she buys. As a result it is always a joy to work with companies there, because the designs and the products they send to Copyrights for approval are usually of excellent quality – and only occasionally do we have to correct their use of English. One amusing instance comes to mind: on a Paddington Bear item received from one of Copyright's Japanese licensees in the 1980s, the design showed Paddington sitting with a marmalade jar, and the text below read 'Happiness comes in pot'.

By the early 1990s, the programme had grown to eighty-eight licensees in the United Kingdom, fifty-two in the United States, and eight in Japan. In Europe there were twenty, in Australia thirty-one, and in South Africa two, in comparison with none in 1984. There were still none in South-East Asia. But the total number of licensees had grown from twenty-five in 1984 to 201 in 1993.

Some of the UK licensees in 1993 were Babychoice, who produced plastic feeding bottles and melamine bowls and plates for young children; British Tissues, who made kitchen towels and tissues; and Hamilton McBride, who made adult-size bedding for older children. Lakefield Marketing managed the Peter Rabbit and Friends shops, and in 1991 Lakes Story had opened 'The World of Beatrix Potter' attraction in Bowness.

In Europe, Hennes and Mauritz, the Swedish-based retailers, produced a wide range of Beatrix Potter children's clothing with innovative motifs and designs. A Dutch company called Interstat produced very attractive stationery, utilising designs around the edges of the items, in patterns. In the sewing category, we licensed Permin, a needlecraft company in Denmark. Resin figurines made by Enesco came in at this time. More detail can be achieved in resin than in ceramic, and the figurines were cheaper because they were made in the Far East. Sadly, this has been one of the reasons why Royal Doulton is at present in such a poor state, the other being that Britain really cannot support two major ceramics companies. Wedgwood is certainly the stronger one at the moment.

In 1993, two important events took place. Firstly, the Beatrix Potter tales were animated and Copyrights therefore licensed a selection of products featuring images from the animation. These were moderately successful at the time, but the animation in many respects had a harsher image when it came to merchandise, and it was not very flexible. We do not license the animation images very much today. The second event in 1993 was, of course, the centenary of the creation of Peter Rabbit in the picture letter which Beatrix Potter wrote to Noel Moore in 1893. Border Fine Arts produced a range of centenary resin figurines for the collector market. SAC (Traditional Games) asked if it could manufacture the game that Beatrix herself had thought about, but which had never actually been produced before. Lakefield Marketing created a centenary tee-shirt, and in Australia Cos brought out special bags and aprons, and Barrymore a centenary book and bag. At about this time, it was also decided to use some of Beatrix Potter's other wonderful artwork, including her botanical paintings and landscapes and this licensing programme was called 'Beatrix Potter's Country World'.

In the United States, there were several new licensees. Michel & Co makes stationery and resin frames in California. This gift company was owned and run by a designer, but she sold out in 1999, since when sadly the company has not produced the same sort of innovative designs. Nathan and Co are a fabric company; All Night Media produced rubber stamps; and Bryan made dresses. Mead Johnson, a very well known pharmaceutical company, took a licence to use a Peter Rabbit image on its infant formula, Enfamil. Feeding bottles were manufactured by Evenflo. A company called Warren Featherbone produced very fine Christening clothes, utilising Beatrix Potter's autograph embroidered in silk on the sleeves – an example of very subtle branding which has also been taken up by some of the designer labels. Mattel asked if it could market a Peter Rabbit Barbie doll. Barbie is extremely popular in the United States and there are many Barbie collectors, so it was decided to give them a licence. 'My Peter Rabbit Barbie' comes with a little Peter Rabbit book, and has images of Peter Rabbit printed on her dress. She went

The Collector Edition of Barbie and her copy of *The Tale of Peter Rabbit*

into the collectable market, and she was Mattel's second-best-selling collectable Barbie doll when she was introduced. R John Wright produced a very expensive hand-made mohair Peter Rabbit toy, with a retail price of around £500, in a limited edition of 1,500 worldwide. This is a really beautiful collectors' item.

In Japan, QP took a licence to use Peter Rabbit to promote its mayonnaise. Peter Rabbit was also used in bank promotions; this is very common in Japan, where a lot of banks use characters to promote their services. Seiko produced pretty watches, and Sekiguchi resin figurines. Bon is a very good puzzle manufacturer, and Denny's did promotions for restaurants. Waterford Wedgwood was distributing Wedgwood china in Japan and developing its own packaged tea.

By 2002 there were ninety-seven licensees in the United Kingdom, and seventy-three in North America. There were seventy-two licensees in Japan, which is much more in keeping with the size of that market. Europe had seventy-one licensees, Australia forty-three, and there were thirty-two in South-East Asia – in Thailand, Taiwan, Korea, Hong Kong and in mainland China. Copyrights also has twelve licensees in other parts of the world, such as South Africa.

In the UK, Good Directions now makes beautiful garden figurines, which have been very successful largely as a result of the huge popularity of gardening products in the last few years. Royal Doulton's licence finished at the end of 2002; Enesco has acquired Border Fine Arts and now manufactures all the ceramic figurines. Wedgwood is still a licensee for porcelain nurseryware and other china products.

A point came in the late 1990s when either Beatrix Potter's original artwork was going to have to be distorted out of all recognition in order to meet the requirements of modern manufacturing techniques, or there would not be as much merchandise on the market in the future. Frederick Warne and Copyrights, both being commercial organisations, opted to do something about this, and 'New Look Peter Rabbit' was the result. Purists might construe this as a controversial move, but Beatrix Potter did say that the products were a 'side show', not the main show. They are ephemeral, they change, and they are dictated in the final instance by the market place; and the market place demands greater movement in design and more colour.

It took a long time for Frederick Warne to develop the New Look artwork. It considered what Beatrix herself would be doing with Peter Rabbit if she were still alive, and even painting, today. Technology has moved on, with the availability of different paints and more varieties of paper, and even the way students are taught to paint is different today. The New Look artwork is particularly targeted at babies and young mothers, for the nursery is now perceived as a fashion extension. For babies there are products which are more user-friendly for today's young mums. Wedgwood and Enesco are using New Look artwork on their products. Mepal in Holland makes melamine dinnerware and feeding items, and nursery bedding is created by Clair De Lune. Hennes and Mauritz in Sweden are also doing New Look clothing and bibs. In America Luv n' Care makes a range of feeding accessories, and Mayfair manufactures clothing.

The 'Classic Art' is still being used on many products. In Japan Yamaka is making Chinese-style bowls and dishes for Chinese and Japanese food. In Asia design tastes are very different from Western ones, and a character like Peter Rabbit can be used in all sorts of areas which would seem quite strange here, so it is not unusual to see Peter Rabbit on frying pans or on casserole dishes.

Over the last twenty years, shopping habits have changed all over the world. People used to go to a department store for nursery bedding, but in America today department stores do not stock it any more, for it took up too much space and did not give the stores the sales per square foot that they wanted. Today people in the United States buy bedding from a Babies 'R' Us or from a Wal-Mart store. The pattern of shopping has changed and consumers now shop everywhere, so you might also see BMWs or Cadillacs in a Wal-Mart parking lot.

The year 2002 marked the hundredth anniversary of the first commercial publication of *The Tale of Peter Rabbit* by Frederick Warne, and in order to celebrate this, Copyrights licensed some special centenary products. For example, the famous German toy bear company, Steiff, produced a replica of Beatrix Potter's 1903 Peter Rabbit doll. Wedgwood designed special products for the centenary; Border Fine Arts produced centenary resin figurines; and in the

Steiff's centenary reproduction of Beatrix Potter's 1903 Peter Rabbit doll

United States R John Wright created a 'Peter Rabbit and the Gardener' piece. Also in the United States, Frankford Candy now produces Easter confectionery. Rashti makes up wonderful baskets of flannels, feeding items, brushes and combs as gifts for baby showers and Christenings, and Teleflora has been enormously successful at doing Christening and Mother's Day bouquets. In Japan, Asahi makes cutlery and Azuma glassware. Citizen is a new watch manufacturer. Koizumi Sangyo makes desks and other furniture, and Konica has produced Peter Rabbit cameras. Sekisui does a wonderful collection of plastic bath accessories, which are widely used in Japanese homes.

By mid-2002 Copyrights had 400 Peter Rabbit licensees worldwide, in comparison with the twenty-five in 1984. This is actually a relatively small number when compared with, for example, the character of Winnie-the-Pooh, where the licensing programme covers about 1,500 companies. Beatrix Potter products remain special to consumers, who have to seek them out.

What does the future hold for Beatrix Potter licensing? Copyrights is planning to carry the licensing programme to new territories – such as South America and South-East Asia, perhaps even to Beijing and Shanghai. And Peter Rabbit will continue to enchant new fans. Parents in all parts of the world and from all walks of life will continue to decorate their nurseries with bedding, lamps, clothing, toys and a choice of hundreds of collectables. The licensing programme, like that naughty Peter, is set to run and run.

Unlike Winnie the pooh it is still essentially the original illustrations - not disneyfied and therefore doesn't cannabalise original books, instead enhances them.

Goes out of copyright at the end of this year - what will happen then?

Gardening with Beatrix Potter

PETER PARKER

IT ALL BEGINS in a garden: a large, attractive kitchen garden overseen by an elderly and ferocious man with wire-framed spectacles and a long white beard. Row upon row of cabbages, onions, peas and potatoes are grown here, along with lettuces, French beans, radishes and parsley. There are blackcurrant bushes, gooseberries protected by netting, a cucumber frame. There is an ornamental pond with lilies, irises and goldfish in it and nasturtiums trailing across its stone surround, and there is a well-stocked and neatly ordered tool-shed with terracotta pots of pink and red geraniums on the windowsill. Chrysanthemum cuttings are growing in other pots outside. Numerous paths divide the beds, some bordered by well-clipped box hedging. At least two ways lead in and out of this garden: a narrow wooden gate set in a long hedge, with woodland beyond, and a door in a red-brick wall which is kept securely locked. The garden is plagued by rabbits.

For many people, Mr. McGregor's garden is the first one that they ever encounter in a book. A little later on, perhaps, they will get to know another enclosed garden with a firmly locked door, Misselthwaite Manor in Yorkshire, the setting of Frances Hodgson Burnett's *The Secret Garden*. Mr. McGregor's garden, however, provides our introduction to horticulture. It also introduces the whole world of Beatrix Potter.

Mr. McGregor's garden was further plagued by rabbits in *The Tale of Benjamin Bunny* and *The Tale of the Flopsy Bunnies*, and as these books grew in popularity, readers poring over Beatrix Potter's finely detailed illustrations became keen to find out where exactly Mr. McGregor kept his garden, where the gate was that Peter Rabbit scrambled under, where it was that Peter and his cousin Benjamin left little clog marks all over the recently seeded lettuce bed. This was not really the point, as Potter herself made clear. 'Peter [Rabbit] was so composite and scattered in locality that I have found it troublesome to explain its various sources', she wrote with characteristic asperity.

If the vegetable garden & wickit [sic] gate were anywhere it was at Lingholme near Keswick; but it would be vain to look for it there, as a firm of landscape gardeners did away with it, and laid it out anew with paved walks etc. . . . The lily pond in Peter was at Tenby, S[outh] Wales. The fir tree and some wood backgrounds were near Keswick. . . . Peter Rabbit's potting shed and the actual geraniums were in Hertfordshire – but what does it matter?

One can add that details of the garden as it appears in *The Tale of the Flopsy Bunnies* come from Gwaynynog, a house near Denbigh in north Wales belonging to Beatrix Potter's uncle, while most of the illustrations for *The Tale of Benjamin Bunny* depict the garden at Fawe Park, Keswick, where Potter spent the summer of 1903. 'I think I have done every imaginable rabbit background, & miscellaneous sketches as well – about 70!' she wrote to her publisher. 'I hope you will like them, though rather scribbled'. This was unduly modest and *The Tale of Benjamin Bunny* is undoubtedly the most beautifully illustrated of the three rabbit books.

One result of a 'scribble' shows the planks laid alongside some vegetable beds under a sunny red-brick wall, along which Peter and Benjamin walk, observed by some dormice eating cherry-stones. Potter tidied up the rather rickety planks, altered the perspective and framed the composition, transforming a charming watercolour study into a book illustration.

Amongst other preliminary sketches was a beautiful drawing of a red carnation, which at one point she intended using as the basis for the book's

Beatrix Potter's 1903 sketch, and her finished picture for *The Tale of Benjamin Bunny*

frontispiece. In the end she replaced this with a picture of Old Mrs. Rabbit in her shop, but her labours did not go to waste. A red carnation features in one of the illustrations, as a nervous Peter drops his onions down a flight of steps. Mr. McGregor grows other dianthus, too, since in another illustration Benjamin is seen sporting a purloined pink – possibly *Dianthus* 'Gran's Favourite' – in his buttonhole. Benjamin continued to be associated with carnations, just as Peter's flower was the pelargonium, each rabbit being depicted with his floral emblem on the end-papers Potter designed for the entire series of books. So, despite the careful preliminary drawings Potter made, Mr. McGregor's garden is not only a composite, it is a composite considerably altered by imagination and invention. Just how much Potter changed things from her models – far more so than the plank walk – can be seen by comparing a painting of the Tenby garden, done in April 1990, and the lily pond as it appears in *The Tale of Peter Rabbit*. The original pond appears to have been set in a path, is circular and surrounded by some sort of low hedge. It also has a rocky island in the middle of it and is quite different in style from Mr. McGregor's more formal pool, although both of them contain goldfish.

To ask where the original garden was is a bit like asking who was the model for Mr. McGregor. I have always thought he bore a marked resemblance to Lytton Strachey, but as yet neither scholars of Bloomsbury nor those of Beatrix Potter have uncovered a link between these two sardonic writers. It is obvious, as Oscar Wilde might have said, that their social spheres were widely different. 'I never knew a gardiner [sic] named "McGregor",' Potter insisted. 'Several bearded horticulturists have resented the nick-name; but I do not know how it came about.'

A far more interesting question it seems to me, and one which I have never seen addressed, is: who really owned this garden? Although it is always referred to as 'Mr. McGregor's garden', it surely does not belong to the old man with the long beard. It is, as we have seen, a very extensive garden indeed, and there is no way Mr. and Mrs. McGregor could ever consume the amount of produce grown there. (If there were ever any little McGregors – which for some reason strikes me as unlikely – they must have long since flown the parental coop.) With his corduroy trousers, hobnail boots, shapeless old jacket and extraordinary hat, Mr. McGregor does not look the sort of man to own so substantial a garden. His house, which appears in *The Tale of the Flopsy Bunnies*, is extremely modest by comparison.

In one of Potter's preliminary sketches, Mr. McGregor has his sleeves rolled up, something no Edwardian gentleman ever did while there were staff on hand. Unfortunately his beard is so luxuriant that you cannot make out what is going on beneath it, but I strongly suspect that his shirt has no collar. If anyone remains in any doubt about the McGregors' social status, then you need only look at the illustration of Mrs. McGregor which Potter was forced to drop from *The Tale of Peter Rabbit*. The old woman proffering a pie containing Peter's unfortunate father is clearly not a lady, any more than her husband, whose uncouth table manners are quite apparent in this painting, is a gentleman.

The point is that as far as the trespassing rabbits are concerned, Mr. McGregor might as well own the garden – and in this (as in much else, not least his uncertain temper) he always reminded me of my own grandparents' gardener, a Mr Lionel Thomas. Mr Thomas seemed extraordinarily ancient to me as a small boy in the early 1960s, and with his drooping yellow moustache, flat cap, striped collarless shirt, shiny navy-blue waistcoat with its watch-chain slung across it, he remained very much an Edwardian. He regarded me much as Mr. McGregor regarded Peter Rabbit – and, I regret to say, with good reason. (Start-Rite sandals make as much mess of a seedbed as clogs do.) If he did not actually chase me with a rake it was not because he was less fearsome than Peter Rabbit's adversary, merely less sprightly.

This is not simply a self-indulgent autobiographical digression. For many children, as for Peter Rabbit, gardens are a place for exploration and foraging, possibly against the express instructions of a parent. Peter and Benjamin are not the only juvenile characters in Potter's book who get into mischief in a garden. Which child has not wandered round a kitchen garden on a summer's afternoon, picking and eating fruit and vegetables? No wonder we all identify with Peter and Benjamin.

Like all children, however, Peter grows up and he becomes – appropriately enough – a nurseryman. In *The Tale of the Flopsy Bunnies* he seems to have acquired a large plot of land. His principal crop appears to be cabbages, but in a drawing that appeared only in early editions, a sign outside the garden announced Peter's other business

Beatrix Potter's original 1909 illustration for *The Tale of the Flopsy Bunnies*

interests: 'Peter Rabbit & Mother, Florists. Gardens neatly razed. Borders devastated by the Night or Year'. This nice little joke was subsequently dropped because the notice would have had to be re-lettered every time the book was translated into a foreign language.

A London child, Potter was brought up in the deceptively-named Bolton Gardens, a rather drab Kensington square. Frequently unwell, she did not make many excursions beyond Kensington Gardens, although Camfield Place, her grandfather's house in Hertfordshire, had grounds laid out by Capability Brown, and so provided her with a taste of the natural world, albeit one carefully manicured. A memoir she wrote of Camfield in about 1891 mentions no flowerbeds, only lawns and trees, mostly planted by Brown, but with later additions by her grandfather. She rather unfairly compared her grandfather's 'muddled and overcrowded efforts' with Brown's scheme.

Family holidays in Scotland provided further glimpses of her natural world. It was this world, with its wild flowers and fungi and animals, that particularly appealed to her, and initially she was more interested in botany than in horticulture. It is significant, however, that when she began to develop her imagination and to picture animals inhabiting a world not unlike the human one, one of the activities her creatures pursued was gardening. In the summer of 1891 she made an exquisitely detailed study of 'The Rabbits' Potting Shed'. Surrounded by assorted rakes, forks, spades, besoms and dibbers, two rabbits – one in a gardener's apron, the other in a jacket not unlike Peter's – are depicted potting up pelargonium and fuchsia cuttings. At the same time she made sketches of a rabbit setting off to work with a spade on his shoulder and a trug on one arm, past pots of pelargoniums and pansies. (These ideas were eventually used for *Peter Rabbit's Almanac* in 1929.) Two years later, she depicted guinea-pig gardeners on their way to work, hurrying along beside a bed of lettuce.

Potter's ideal of a garden was her uncle's one at Gwaynynog, which she described in her journal in 1895: 'The garden is very large, two-thirds surrounded by a red-brick wall with many apricots, and an inner circle of old grey apple trees on wooden espaliers. It is very productive but not tidy, the prettiest kind of garden, where bright old fashioned flowers grow amongst the currant bushes.' In her fairy story, *Llewellyn's Well*, written in 1911 or 1912, Potter provided another description of Gwaynynog:

> The garden lay behind the house, inside a mossy red brick wall. It was filled with apricots, apples and pears; and peaches in their season. In Summer there were white and damask roses, and the smell of thyme and musk. In Spring there were green gooseberries and throstles, and the flowers they call ceninen [wild daffodils].

And leeks and cabbages also grew in that garden; and between long straight grass alleys, and apple-trained espaliers, there were beds of strawberries, and mint and sage. And great holly trees and a thicket of nuts; it was a great big garden.

Another ideal was Lakefield, the house at Sawrey where Potter first stayed in 1896. A painting of the garden she did there was titled simply: 'An English Garden'. She described Sawrey 'as nearly perfect a little place as I ever lived in' and commented approvingly on 'the flowery little gardens' of the village. It was Sawrey, of course, that provided her with further models for the gardens in her books.

'The Rabbits' Potting Shed', Bedwell Lodge, 1891

The most floriferous of all the books is *The Tale of the Pie and the Patty-Pan*, which was originally produced in a new, larger format and so gave Potter the chance of painting some more detailed illustrations. Duchess's front garden, based on Buckle Yeat in Sawrey, provides the little Pomeranian with a vast array of flowers against which to pose and from which to gather an enormous bouquet to take around to Cousin Ribby when she goes to tea. Potter made detailed sketches of these gardens and then adapted them for her own purposes.

I once spent a long and happy time attempting to identify the individual flowers growing in this garden and thought I spotted antirrhinums, linaria, Welsh poppies, calendula, helichrysum, centaurea, mallow, sweet-william, Turk's-cap lilies and a pink standard rose. I wrote as much in an article for the gardening journal *Hortus*, and it was subsequently reprinted in the Beatrix Potter Society *Newsletter* [Nos. 64 and 65], thus giving ample opportunity for contradiction from two sets of experts. I received no complaints, which is I think a tribute to Potter's botanical accuracy.

Duchess's garden, like Mr. McGregor's, is in fact a composite: in another picture, Duchess stands amongst some very fine tiger lilies, and this garden, and the handsome Georgian door, are taken from the Post Office on the opposite side of the street from Buckle Yeat. The real people who presumably owned this second garden, and their cats, are reduced to mere pencilled ghosts in this preliminary sketch, since Potter was chiefly interested in the horticultural and architectural details. These form the perfect backdrop for Duchess as she sets off on her errand to substitute a veal and ham pie for the mouse one she fears has been prepared for her by her hostess.

Potter's taste for unkempt gardens was overcome by her sense of design, and she made the planting a little more tidy in the picture than it was in life. For example, the glaucous-leafed opium poppies in the original sketch were in pink bloom, providing something of a clash with the orange tiger-lilies. In the finished picture, the plants have buds and seedheads but no frilled flowers. When I first tried to identify what the lilies were underplanted with, I consulted the well-known nurserywoman Carol Klein. She tentatively suggested white perennial musk mallow, *Malva moschata* 'Alba'; but they could be the cranesbill *Geranium macrorrhizum* 'Album' or even one of those pretty, low-growing evening primroses. As with the gardens, perhaps it is pointless trying to identify such plants authoritatively. Potter knew her plants, but she was, after all, making a picture here rather than a botanical study. When

Beatrix Potter's sketch of the Post Office in Sawrey which inspired Duchess's garden in *The Tale of the Pie and the Patty-Pan*

writing my article for *Hortus*, I hazarded a guess that the plants in the illustration on page 41 of *The Tale of Benjamin Bunny* 'might be red lupins, or possibly valerian'. I subsequently discovered that they were in fact snapdragons. 'I think the snap dragon is much better for toning down,' she told Warne, '& I have made those rabbits larger.' It may have been the scale that misled me in the first place – but in my defence I would suggest that nature has been sacrificed to art in this instance. Snapdragons are undoubtedly one of the 'bright old fashioned flowers' that Potter favoured, and I think that the rather dull red of those in that illustration owed more to her sense of composition than to her botanical exactness.

Making pictures was an important part of Potter's work. When she was trying to persuade a somewhat reluctant Norman Warne of the merits of a book about Mr. Jeremy Fisher, she wrote: 'I'm afraid you don't like *frogs*, but it would make pretty pictures with water-forget-me-nots, lilies, etc.' Pretty pictures were what children wanted, perhaps, but Potter always put the right plants in the right places. She made good her promise to Warne, filling the pictures for Jeremy Fisher not only with lilies and forget-me-nots, but also with yellow ranunculus, violets, cowslips, daisies, and assorted reeds and rushes. Jeremy's boat, a lily-pad, is kept tied up to what Potter describes in the text merely as a water-plant, but in the accompanying illustration it is easy to identify the clearly ribbed leaves and airy panicles of the water plantain *Alisma plantago-aquatica*.

The other garden in *The Tale of the Pie and the Patty-Pan* belongs to Ribby, the cat with whom Duchess is having the worrying tea. Once again, it is Duchess who hogs the limelight, posing in front of Ribby's porch brandishing her enormous bouquet. The porch was that of Lakefield Cottage, owned appropriately enough by Lakefield's own Mr. McGregor, James Rogerson, who acted as gardener and caretaker at the big house. Potter copied the porch very accurately, and the planting is exactly as it was in the original. Dark purple *Clematis*

Alisma plantago-aquatica in *The Tale of Mr. Jeremy Fisher*

'Jackmanii' and scarlet *Tropaeolum speciosum* (the flame creeper) scrambles over it, and its slate-topped shelves bear pots of red geranium.

It was while Potter was working on *The Tale of the Pie and the Patty-Pan* and was therefore absorbed in Sawrey that she decided to buy her own property in the district, Hill Top Farm. 'The garden is very overgrown & untidy,' she told Millie Warne a few months after her purchase, 'I hope next time you come it will be straighter, I have got the quarryman making walks & beds, it would not have been work for a visitor! but it will be a great pleasure to show you the result some day.' Unfortunately, the initial work did not improve matters much. 'The new works though doubtless an improvement are painfully *new*,' she told Millie. 'Instead of the old winding road – with a tumble down wall covered with polypody [the common, bracken-like fern] – there is a straight wide road & a very bare wall. Also heaps of soil everywhere & new railings, they would show less if they were tarred. Things very soon become moss grown at the Lakes, it will mend itself in a year or two.' Potter was already learning the one virtue needed above all other by gardeners: patience. She liked old walls and started collecting plants for the newly mended one, even going so far as to rescue 'some pretty wall-rue fern' from a nearby bridge that was being demolished.

Much of the new garden was taken up with a lawn. 'I believe the word "tennis" *was* mentioned,' Potter complained, 'but I have never played it, so it conveyed nothing particular to my mind. I could not think why he [the workman] was taking such a time & now I discover a thing big enough for playing football! half the garden.' She was having none of this, 'I was just in time to stop him sowing it today,' she continued, by now well into her stride as a practical countrywoman. 'I have told the farmer to plant potatos [sic] all over it this season, as I don't feel inclined to pay any more wages at present for altering it.'

What Potter had in mind for her own garden may be seen in the illustrations for *The Tale of Tom Kitten*, which is set at Hill Top. A winding path leads from the house, owned for the purposes of the story by Mrs. Tabitha Twitchit, through a very pretty cottage garden. Some beautifully espaliered apple trees are in blossom to Mrs. Twitchit's left, growing against some sturdy trellis work and underplanted with cottage garden favourites. On the other side of the path are pinks, narcissi and a rather blurred purple plant I should like to think was *Nepeta*, catmint. In the background, the porch is wreathed in a large-flowered clematis, and in another more detailed illustration, we see that *Tropaeolum* is also grown there, just as it was in *The Tale of the Pie and the Patty-Pan*. The reason for this, I think, is that Ribby is Tabitha Twitchit's cousin, and

I like to imagine these gardening felines swapping plants, as all good gardeners do.

By now Potter herself was learning fast about all aspects of gardening. She was most indignant that the council had employed a man to use all the horse manure left by passing traffic in the road outside the house to fill potholes, a practice she described as 'both nasty & illegal'. By law, or at any rate custom, horse dung was the property of the person outside whose house it had been left. Presumably Potter managed to assert her rights, since she later regaled Millie Warne with news that she was 'in course of putting liquid manure on the apple trees!! It is a most interesting performance with a long scoop,' she added, making a sketch of herself absorbed in this task.

Mrs. Tabitha Twitchit's garden in *The Tale of Tom Kitten* is Beatrix Potter's garden at Hill Top

'I have got a large bed in the garden prepared by digging,' she reported in September 1906.

> I am going to the nursery at Windermere this week to choose some bushes; I am being inundated with offers of plants! It is very kind of people; and as it really is the right time to thin & replant, I don't feel such a robber of the village gardens. There is a quarry-man who lives on the road to the ferry who has got some most splendid phloxes, they will look nice between the laurels while the laurels are small. I shall plant the lilies between the azaleas. I have got a saxifrage here that would be just what you want, but I do not know its variety name. I will try to find out – my cousin gave me some bits, it was planted in a pot about this much [she provides a drawing] in August & in that short time it has completely covered the soil in the top of the pot like small moss. I might as well bring one of the pots back with me for you to look at. I have been very busy planting cuttings of rock plants on the top of the garden wall – I have got cuttings of "white" rock which have crimson & purple flowers.

Soon she was telling Millie Warne:

> My news is all gardening at present, & supplies. I went to see an old lady at Windermere, & impudently took a large basket & trowel with me. She had the most untidy overgrown garden I ever saw. I got nice things in handfuls without any shame, amongst others a bundle of lavender slips, if they "strike" they will

be enough for a lavender hedge; and another bundle of violet suckers, I am going to set some of them in the orchard. My cousin at Windermere sent a hamper of big roots, rather coarse things but they will do nicely amongst the shrubs and there were some nice things amongst them, Japanese anemones & sweet williams. Mrs Satterthwaite says stolen plants always grow, I stole some "honesty" yesterday, it was put to be burnt in a heap of garden refuse! I have had something out of nearly every garden in the village. . . . I have planted Mr Dipnalls lilies most carefully, in a mixture of sand, old mortar & peat. I ought to do well with lilies, having a supply of black peat soil.

Lilies do not feature in the illustrations for *The Tale of Tom Kitten* – perhaps Potter's confidence was misplaced – but as we have seen, plenty of other cottage garden favourites do. Expecting guests for afternoon tea, Mrs. Twitchit dresses her kittens in their best party clothes, and then 'unwisely turned them out into the garden, to be out of the way while she made hot buttered toast'. Alas, the young Twitchits, like Peter Rabbit before them, ignore all their mother's injunctions, and rather than remaining clean and tidy, immediately start chasing the butterflies flitting amongst the violas and pinks. Moppet and Mittens get 'green smears' all over their pinafores and drop their tuckers into the road as they scramble up through ferns and rhododendrons on to the well-planted garden wall. (Potter mentioned buying rhododendron bushes in October 1906, the year before the book was published.) Tom fares as badly as his sisters: 'He came up the rockery by degrees, breaking the ferns, and shedding buttons right and left. He was all in pieces when he reached the top of the wall. Moppet and Mittens tried to pull him together; his hat fell off, and the rest of his buttons burst.'

In the illustration of the three kittens, who have lost rather more than their mittens, it is obvious that Potter's plan to plant up the old wall has succeeded. Ferns stick out of the wall just below their paws. Also, in the background, are the richly manured fruit trees. Incidentally, why is it that the animals in the books seem to lose their clothes whenever they venture into a garden? I'm sure that someone somewhere must be writing a dissertation on this fruitful subject.

The farm garden at Hill Top features in *The Tale of Jemima Puddle-Duck*, which reintroduces a character from *The Tale of Tom Kitten*. Jemima is sent to the garden by the sandy-whiskered gentleman, supposedly to gather ingredients for a savoury omelette: 'Sage and thyme, and mint and two onions, and some parsley'. 'Jemima Puddle-duck was a simpleton,' Potter comments uncharitably: 'not even the mention of sage and onion made her suspicious' – and she provides a charming illustration of the silly bird in the farm garden happily 'nibbling off snippets of all the different sorts of herbs that are used for stuffing roast duck'.

One of the book's jokes is that Jemima never recognises the 'mighty civil and handsome' gentleman for what he is. Despite the fact that he has a bushy tail and 'black prick ears', she fails to recognise his true nature beneath its elegant disguise of a tweed knickerbocker suit and cherry-coloured waistcoat. However, the foxgloves surrounding the tree stump, on which he is first discovered reading a newspaper, suggest to us, if not to poor dim Jemima, his true identity.

By now Potter was spending much of her earnings on gardening and was asking her publisher when money was due because she wanted to plan ahead. For Christmas 1909, she let Harold Warne know in advance about a suitable Christmas present: 'I wish Frue would give me a book about pruning roses,' she told him, adding characteristically: 'there is nothing like being candid'. She was becoming quite an expert now, and proffering advice where once she had sought it. 'I wonder if you have room for any phlox,' she asked Millie Warne in October 1910, 'it is the time of year for dividing herbaceous plants, mine have all grown into a tangle.'

Jemima Puddle-duck fails to identify the gentleman sitting amongst the foxgloves

Potter's characters continued to garden, most notably the guinea-pigs in *Cecily Parsley's Nursery Rhymes.*

> We have a little garden,
>   A garden of our own,
> And every day we water there
>   The seeds that we have sown.
>
> We love our little garden,
>   And tend it with such care,
> You will not find a faded leaf
>   Or blighted blossom there.

In fact the guinea-pigs appear to be jobbing gardeners, working to the orders of a stern old gentleman, who inspects their labours through a pair of pince-nez.

The unsupervised guinea-pigs in *Cecily Parsley's Nursery Rhymes*, 1922

This is a variation of the drawing already mentioned that Potter did back in 1891. The guinea pigs look a lot happier when unsupervised. Left to their own devices and relieved of the job of preparing the soil, the guinea-pigs grew regale lilies, blue lupins, pink roses and what seems to be *Linaria dalmatica*, a pretty little cottage-garden plant with small yellow snapdragon flowers and glaucous foliage.

When Beatrix Potter married William Heelis in 1913, the couple decided to live in Castle Cottage on a farm which she had acquired four years earlier. The garden there was in the style she always favoured, 'a regular old fashioned farm garden', as she described it to one correspondent, 'with a box hedge round the flower bed, and moss roses and pansies and black currants & strawberries and peas – and big sage bushes for Jemima, but onions always do badly.' She also grew what she called 'tall white bell flowers' (probably some sort of campanula), phlox, Michaelmas daisies and chrysanthemums. After Christmas the first snowdrops appeared: 'they grow wild and come up all over the garden & orchard, and in some of the woods'.

Even when she stopped writing the 'damned little books', she found little enough time for her garden. It was a case of 'survival of the fitest [sic],' she told her cousin Caroline Clark (née Hutton) in December 1930. 'It always seems too wet or too busy at the right time for digging over – consequently I just let the plants alone until they *have* to be divided, and small things like gentians have got crowded out.' It was pretty ambitious to be growing gentians at all, since they are temperamental even by the standards of alpine plants, but

Potter now regarded herself as an expert and advised: 'I think they will stand wet if you mix pebbles or old lime with the soil, for drainage.'

Towards the end of her life, Beatrix Potter acquired yet another garden when she bought Belmount Hall near Hawkshead. This was a walled garden of over an acre. She complained that the fan-trained fruit trees were 'in the last stage of old age' but she planted 'clematis against them, and some shrubs, such as ceanothus, between, to gradually grow into their place'. She asked her cousin Caroline: 'Is chimomanthus fragrans [wintersweet] a bush that would grow? I have witch hazel, and shrubby spiraeas, and syringas. I remember you said you were going in for shrubs – and for the same reason. I should like to plant some bushes that might grow on at Belmount Hall without much attention? The garden is not seriously weedy. It is carpeted [sic] with jonquils & spring flowers.' She asked Caroline to send the names of any shrubs she thought suitable, on a postcard.

However expert a gardener Beatrix Potter may have become, and however much we wander around Sawrey with a National Trust guidebook in one hand and *The Tale of the Pie and the Patty-Pan* in the other, I come back to my original point, one I think Potter herself would endorse. It is in vain to look for the 'real gardens', as she said. By their very nature, gardens are ephemeral. We can plan and plant and tend, but all our work may be altered or swept away by those who come after us. In her letters and *Journal* Beatrix Potter made it clear what her favourite sort of garden would be, and to some extent she achieved it at Hill Top; but even here one feels that with no guinea-pigs to tend it, there must have been the occasional faded leaf or blighted blossom. One of the great virtues of art is that it can transform nature and overcome these shortfalls. It can sort out the perspective, fill in the awkward gaps, tidy away anything unsightly. Mr. McGregor's garden remains an *ideal*, and ideals tend to be found in books rather than real life. In 2002 in *The Daily Telegraph* magazine there was a feature about an Italianate garden in Wales. The owner was also planning a vegetable garden and she said she wanted it to be just like Mr. McGregor's. I know what she meant, but at the same time I wonder what the end result will be. Not, one hopes, like the garden at the Chelsea Flower Show a few years back, which purported to be Peter Rabbit's garden but was, to put it politely, merely a crude approximation, complete with some very nasty garden ornaments supposedly representing Potter's characters. The real gardens of Beatrix Potter are the ones to be found in the books and are not subject to change or decay. One hundred years on, we can still step into Mr. McGregor's garden and find it exactly as it was – or, perhaps, as it never was.

Index

Page numbers in **bold type** refer to illustrations. Since the whole of this volume is devoted to aspects of Beatrix Potter's life and work she does not have an Index entry.

Adventures of the Rabbit Called Peter, 71; **71**
Adventures of Two Dutch Dolls and a 'Golliwogg', The, 19
Ahlberg, Janet and Allan, 42
Alksnėnas, Viltaras, 81; **85**
Alice's Adventures in Wonderland (Lewis Carroll), 14, 26
Anning Bell, Robert, 16; **22**
Appley Dapply's Nursery Rhymes, 38

Bairn Books, The, 24; **24**
Ballantyne, R.M., 13
Banbury Cross and other Nursery Rhymes, 17
Banbury Cross Series, the, 16, 18, 19, 20
Bannerman, Helen, 19, 22, 24, 25, 26; **21**
Barbie, 92–3; **92**
Basile, Giambattista, 15
Baskerville, John, 33
Beardsley, Aubrey, 16, 17, 18, 22; **17, 22**
Beatrix Potter: Artist, Storyteller and Countrywoman (Judy Taylor), 44
Beckman, Ernst, 15
Bedwell Lodge, Hertfordshire, **101**
Belmount Hall, Hawkshead, 109
Benjamin Bunny, The Tale of, 49, 61, 96, 97–8, 103; **48, 97**
Bewick, Thomas, 32
Blue Fairy Book, The (Andrew Lang), 15

Bodley Head, The, 16
Bolton Gardens, London, 100
Book of Rhymes (1905), 50
Brer Rabbit, 18
Brooke, L. Leslie, 23
Burne-Jones, Sir Edward, 18; **14**
Burnett, Frances Hodgson, 11, 96
Bush, Barbara, 61–2
Butterfly's Ball, The (William Roscoe), 13

Caldecott, Randolph, 14, 18, 19
Calvert, Edward, 24
Calvin, John, 12
Camfield Place, Hertfordshire, 100
Carroll, Lewis, 14, 69, 74
Carrots (Mrs Molesworth), 14
Caslon, William I, 32–4
Castle Cottage, Sawrey, 108–9
Caxton, William, 32
Cecily Parsley's Nursery Rhymes, 38, 107–8; **108**
Chenov, Denis, 71
Chesterton, G.K., 19, 69
Children's Gem Library, The, 24
Children's Library, 15, 19
Cinderella, 18
Clark, Caroline, 108–9
'clogs', 48–9; **48**
Collodi, Carlo, 15
Complete Tales of Beatrix Potter, The, 83
Coolidge, Mrs J. Templeman, 61
Copyrights Group, The, 86–95

110

Crane, Walter, 15, 29
Crosby, Carole, 54–5, 63

Dalguise House, Scotland, 57
Dent, J.M., 16, 24; **17, 22, 24**
Dream Days (Kenneth Grahame), 18
'Dream of Toasted Cheese, A', 44
Dumpy Books for Children, The, 19, 20, 24, 25; **21**

Edgeworth, Maria, 12
Everyman Library, 16
Evans, Edmund, 32
Ewing, Mrs, 13

Fairweather, Ronnie, 40
Fairy Caravan, The, 49, 75
Fawe Park, Keswick, 97
Five Children and It (E. Nesbit), 11
Flopsy Bunnies, The Tale of The, 84, 96, 97, 98, 99–100; **99**
Frazer, Sir James George, 15
'Frog he would a-fishing go, A', 17, 18, 21

gardens and gardening, 96–109; **97, 99, 101, 102, 105, 108**
Ginger and Pickles, The Tale of, 78
Golden Age, The (Kenneth Grahame), 18
Golden Bough, The (Sir James George Frazer), 15
Golliwog books, The, 19, 20; **19**
Grahame, Kenneth, 18, 74
Granville Fell, H., 17
Grebnev, Mikhail, 71
Greenaway, Kate, 13
Grigorieva, O., 71
Grimm's Household Tales, **22**

Guardian of Education, The, 12
Gutenberg, Johann, 30, 37
Gwaynynog, Denbigh, 97, 100–1

Happy Prince and Other Tales, The (Oscar Wilde), 15
Hatano, Isoko, 77
Heelis, William, 108
Henty, G. A., 13
Hildesheimer & Faulkner, 17
Hill Top Farm, Sawrey, 104–7, 109; **105**
History of the Robin Family (Mrs Trimmer), 12
History of the Writings of Beatrix Potter, A (Leslie Linder), 46, 50
Hoatson, Alice, 18
Hobbs, Anne, 44
Hodder and Stoughton, 24
Holden, Violet, 17
Hollindale, Peter, 26, 75
Horn Book, The, 11–12, 61, 62
Horton Hatches the Egg (Dr Seuss), 61
House that Jack Built, The, 17
Housman, A.E., 19
Housman, Laurence, 18
Howes, Justin, 33–4
Hudgens, Sarah, **60**

Inge-Vechtomova, M., 71
Inoh, Hiroshi, 77
Ishii, Momoko, 77–8

Jemima Puddle-Duck, The Tale of, 58, 63, 71, 73, 106–7; **107**
Johnny Town-Mouse, The Tale of, 63
Journal, The (Beatrix Potter), 62, 109
Jungle Books, The (Rudyard Kipling), 18, 20, 26

Just So Stories (Rudyard Kipling), 11, 26

Kalaushin, G., 79
Kelmscott Press, 14, 15, 16, 18; **14**
Keynote Series, The, 16
Kingsley, Charles, 14
Kipling, Rudyard, 11, 18, 20, 77
Kozhemyakina, Galina, 71
Kozlov, Sergei, 69

Lakefield, Sawrey, 101, 103–4
Lane, John, 16, 18
Lang, Andrew, 15
Le Gallienne, Richard, 18
Le Morte D'Arthur (Sir Thomas Malory), 16; **17**
Lear, Linda, 53
Lewis, C.S., 69
Linder, Leslie, 44, 46, 78
Linder Collection, 46
Lingholm(e), Keswick, 97
Linnaean Society, 18
Listener, The, 24
Little Black Sambo, The Story of (Helen Bannerman), 19–20, 23, 25–6; **21**
Little Black Mingo, The Story of (Helen Bannerman), 24, 25; **24**
'little books', the, 30–2, 34–42
Little Coloured Coon, The Story of a, 24, 25
Little Folks' Favourite Library, The, 17, 20
'Little Hedgehog in the Mist, The' (Sergei Kozlov), 69
Little One's Library, The, 24
Little Pig Robinson, The Tale of, 38
Little Princess, A (Frances Hodgson Burnett), 11
Little Sunshine (Dinah Mulock), 14

Little Yellow Yang-Lo, The Story of, 25
Llewellyn's Well, 100

Mack, Robert Ellice, 17, 18
McLean, Ruari, 29, 32
Mahony (Miller), Bertha, 26, 56, 62
Malory, Sir Thomas, 16; **17**
Mathews, Charles Elkin, 16
Maurer, Teresa, 61–2
Max and Carlino (Ernst Beckman), 15
merchandise and licences, 86–95; **88, 92, 94**
Miss Moppet, The Story of, 38
Molesworth, Mrs, 13, 14
Moore, Anne Carroll, 12, 26, 61, 62
Moore, Freda, 21
Moore, Marjorie, 20–1
Moore, Noel, 13, 14, 20, 54, 92
Moore, Norah, **50**
Morris, William, 14, 18, 19, 22; **14, 22**
Moxon, Joseph, 28
Mr. Jeremy Fisher, The Tale of, 50–1, 61, 63, 81, 82, 103; **103**
Mr. Tod, The Tale of, 57
Mrs. Tiggy-Winkle, The Tale of, 63, 70, 71, 74, 75, 79; **71, 72, 80**
Mrs. Tittlemouse, The Tale of, 57, 74, 81, 84
Mudie's Circulating Library, 13
Mulock, Dinah, 14

Narstein, Yuri, 69
National Trust, the, 45, 46
Naughty Kittens and the Ducks Who Lost Their Clothes, The, 75–7; **76**
Nesbit, E., 11, 18, 24
Newbery, John, 13
Nisbet, James & Company, 25

Nister, Ernest, 17–18, 21, 24
Nister's *Holiday Annual*, 18

Obraztsova, O., 70, 80
Okamoto, Kiichi, 75
Oogley Oo Books, 24, 25; **24**
Otsuki, Ruriko, 83

Palmer, Samuel, 24
Pentamerone (Giambattista Basile), 15
Peter Pan (J.M. Barrie), 26
Peter Rabbit, 12, 13, 14, 16, 52, 79, 96
Peter Rabbit, The Tale of, 11–12, 16, 17, 20–4, 25–6, 30, 31, 32, 38, 41, 44, 46–7, 53, 58, 61, 63, 64, 70, 71, 74, 78, 81, 82, 83, 85, 94, 96–7, 98–9; **21, 22, 42, 47, 65–8, 85, 92**
Peter Rabbit Doll, 87, 94; **94**
Peter Rabbit's Almanac, 100
'Peter Rabbit's Garden', exhibition, 52–3
Peter Rabbit's Painting Book, 87; **88**
Peter Rabbit's Race Game, 87, 90
Pie and the Patty-Pan, The Tale of The, 101–2, 103–4, 109; **102**
Piénkowski, Jan, 35
Pigling Bland, The Tale of, 49; **48**
Pinocchio (Carlo Collodi), 15

'Rabbits' Potting Shed, The', 100; **101**
Rawnsley, Canon Hardwicke, 22–3
Reading Beatrix Potter, 54–68; **55, 60, 65–8**
Richards, Grant, 14, 19, 20, 24, 25
Robinson, Charles, 17
Roscoe, Sir Henry, 44
Roscoe, William, 13

Rosebud Series, The, 24
Routledge, Pocket Library, 13

St Herbert's Island, Derwentwater, 49
Saki, 19
Samuel Whiskers, The Tale of, 57
Sawrey, 101–9
Scott, Sir Walter, 12
Secret Garden, The (Frances Hodgson Burnett), 96
Seuss, Dr, 61
Shaw, George Bernard, 18, 19
Skerstonaite, Laima, 79–80
Smith, Janet Adam, 24–5
Soros Foundation, the, 80
Squirrel Nutkin, The Tale of, 41, 49–50, 75, 81; **49, 50**
Stephens, Arthur, 25, 26
Struwwelpeter, 20
Swan Sonnenschein, 24; **24**

Tailor of Gloucester, The, 38, 41, 77–8; **78**
Taylor, Judy, 40, 44
Temple Shakespeare, The, 16
Tenby, Wales, 97, 98
That Naughty Rabbit: Beatrix Potter and Peter Rabbit (Judy Taylor), 40, 87
Timmy Tiptoes, The Tale of, 74
'toadstools', 49–50
Tom Kitten, The Tale of, 73, 74, 75–7, 104–5, 106; **76, 105**
translations, 69–85; **71, 72, 76, 78, 80, 85**
Treasure Seekers, The (E. Nesbit), 19
Treasury of Peter Rabbit and Other Stories, A, 80
Trimmer, Mrs, 12
Tuck, Raphael, 24

Two Bad Mice, The Tale of, 51, 74, 81, 84

Unwin, George, 15
Updike, D.B., 33
Upton, Florence, 15, 19, 20, 22; **19**
Upton, Ruth, 19, 20, 22; **19**

Very Hungry Caterpillar, The (Eric Carl), 35
Victoria and Albert Museum, the, 45, 46

Warne, Eveline, **51**
Warne, Frederick & Company, 22–4, 25, 30–2, 36, 38–42, 44, 45, 50–1, 52, 55, 59, 64, 81, 86, 87, 88, 107–8
Warne, Frederick, the Archive, 43–53
Warne, Fruing, 51, 107
Warne, Harold, 50–1, 107
Warne, Mary, 51, 52
Warne, Millie, 52, 104–6
Warne, Norman, 51, 52, 103
Warne, Winifred, 51; **51**
Water-Babies, The (Charles Kingsley), 14
Watling, Roy, 18
Waugh, Evelyn, 69
Werner, Marian, 54, 63
Whalley, Irene, 44
Wilde, Oscar, 15, 18
Wildsmith, Brian, 35
Wind in the Willows, The (Kenneth Grahame), 26
Wood Beyond the World, The (William Morris), **14**
Woodward, Alice, 17

Yours Affectionately, Peter Rabbit, 77

Zakharenkov, Alexei, 71–2; **72**

The Beatrix Potter Society

The Beatrix Potter Society was founded in 1980 by a group of people professionally involved in the curatorship of Beatrix Potter material. It exists to promote the study and appreciation of the life and works of Beatrix Potter (1866–1943), who was not only author and illustrator of *The Tale of Peter Rabbit* and other classics of children's literature, but also a Natural History artist, diarist, farmer and conservationist – in the latter capacity she was responsible for the preservation of large areas of the Lake District through her gifts to the National Trust.

The Society is a registered charity and its membership is worldwide. Its activities include regular talks and meetings in London and visits to places connected with Beatrix Potter. An annual Linder Memorial Lecture is given each spring to commemorate the contribution made to Beatrix Potter studies by Leslie Linder and his sister Enid. The first of these was given at the Victoria and Albert Museum by Margaret Lane, as Patron of the Society. Biennial Study Conferences are held in the Lake District and Scotland and are attended by Members from around the world.

A quarterly *Newsletter*, issued free to Members, contains articles on a wide range of topics as well as information about meetings and visits, reviews of books and exhibitions, Members' letters, and news of Beatrix Potter collections both in the United Kingdom and elsewhere. The Society also publishes the proceedings of its Study Conferences and other works of original research.

Further information can be obtained from:
The Membership Administrator,
9 Broadfields,
Harpenden,
Herts AL5 2HJ

email: info@beatrixpottersociety.org.uk

or from the Society's website:
www.beatrixpottersociety.org.uk